Kingdom Come

M. R. RENKEMA

ISBN 978-1-64079-382-8 (Paperback)
ISBN 978-1-64079-383-5 (Digital)

Christian Faith Publishing, Inc.
296 Chestnut Street
Meadville, PA 16335
www.christianfaithpublishing.com

Printed in the United States of America

CONTENTS

Chapter 1

ARE YOU READY?

Most people long for something more than a regular life. They dream of belonging to something greater than themselves—the hope of participating in more than ordinary. People look for mission and purpose because we were created for it. We were designed for an adventure of a lifetime.

Adventure looks different for every person, but we have a shared goal. We are made to be healed and whole individuals, living in meaningful community, advancing the Kingdom of Heaven.

Often times, stories of adventures can help us begin our own. They inspire us to find our courage and strength and help us begin to dream of what more we can do. I'd like to look at one famous boy to help you start to see what sort of life is right within your reach.

In 1997, J. K. Rowling published the first Harry Potter book. The adventure begins, and we are introduced to a young boy who doesn't fit in. He feels something is different about him and notices that strange things seem to happen around him. One time, Harry's aunt cut off all his hair because she was frustrated that it never grew in an orderly manner, and it completely grew back overnight. While Harry was running away from some bullies at school, namely, his cousin, Harry suddenly finds himself on the roof and away from harm. Harry often dreams of flying motorcycles but can't remember where he got this absurd idea from. And most famously, a giant piece of glass disappears from a snake exhibit at the zoo in front of Harry and his cousin right after the cousin was being nasty to Harry and right as Harry wished something awful would happen to his cousin.

Harry notices these things but can't explain them, and so he listens and believes the only voices he can hear being spoken over him, those of his aunt and uncle. His aunt and uncle took him in after Harry's parents died, and they are awful people. These two people constantly belittle him. They tell Harry daily that he is nothing and that he is ungrateful and worthless and small. Harry doesn't know that they hate him because his parents were wizards. Harry doesn't even know he is a wizard himself, and so he accepts what his awful relatives say about him as truth.

Then, Harry turns 11. Hogwarts, the School of Witchcraft and Wizardry, begins to reach out to Harry in order to bring him back to the wizarding world by sending him letters. This infuriates his aunt and uncle, and so they keep the life-altering letters away from him. His worldly family has a huge fear of the wizarding world. Hogwarts is persistent however and sends letter after letter, increasing in bulk until it cannot be denied that Hogwarts will do whatever it can to get their message to Harry.

In a last-ditch effort to keep Harry in the shadows, the uncle decides it's time to go far away. They pack up and go to a cabin on a lake in the middle of nowhere. The terrified uncle decides that this cabin is a safe place from the magical school that is pestering his family.

At this point, Hogwarts decides to send someone to retrieve Harry since he is not responding to the letters. Hogwarts elects Hagrid to go out and bring Harry home. Hagrid is an easy pick for this task, as he is the games keeper at Hogwarts and is a very large man since he is a half giant. So, when Hagrid turns up at the cabin, he easily pushes aside the locked door, affectively removing the last physical barrier between Harry and the truth. Hagrid is elated to see Harry again, having known Harry since he was born. Hagrid can't wait to bring Harry home and assumes he knows what is in store. But Harry's aunt and uncle continue to be the last obstacle that stands in Harry's way. Seeing that the boy will follow in his parent's footsteps, seeing that he will become what they consider a freak, the feeble uncle yells at Hagrid in an attempt to keep Harry in the dark.

Though the uncle's protests seem like nothing in comparison to the truth that Hagrid holds, Harry still doesn't see the lies for what they are. Harry himself tells Hagrid that he must be mistaken because how could he, a scrawny kid, be anything more than nothing.

When Hagrid realizes that Harry knows nothing about the wizarding world, he is outraged. Hagrid wants Harry to instantly know the entirety of what kind of life awaits him but doesn't even know where to begin. And so, Hagrid simply utters the truth of Harry's identity, "Harry – yer a wizard."[1]

Harry stammers. He doesn't understand what this means. Could it be? Could he be more than ordinary? Something clicks inside himself, something shifts, and the fog is gone. Harry latches on to the first true thing he has ever heard about himself and never lets go.

The next 7 books are full of Harry learning, training, and growing into who he was made to be. He takes the wizarding world in stride and eagerly learns all he can about the place he was designed for. He sees and smells and tastes and touches things that could only be home. Harry forever leaves behind the lies of his past and runs with abandon into his true self. And on top of it all, he discovers that he is already famous.

When Harry was a baby, his parents died protecting him from the greatest evil wizard of their time. Harry Potter is famous because of his parents' selfless love. Their sacrifice enabled him to defeat death, while he was only an infant. This knowledge gives Harry the resolve and determination to continue the war against the impending darkness. Harry finds deep courage, boldness, and love within himself as he works to release the world from evil.

Harry Potter is a work of fiction, but this illustration is power. This is us. We are in a world that has been trying to keep us in a cupboard under the stairs, and we think it's right because it has been the only voice we have ever heard, because it has been shouting the loudest, and because we didn't know there was another voice. But once we hear the Voice, the Tender One, the one of Love, everything melts off and we run into the world we were made for.

And do you want to hear the truth? Do you want to set your heart on the one thing that is your identity—the thing that calls to you and the thing that the enemy would do everything to keep you from knowing?

You are a child of the One True King.

And the world you belong to is the Kingdom of Heaven.

We are famous not because of anything we did. We are famous because our Father God performed an act of love so deep that His Son became like us, died in our place, and rose again to defeat death once and for all. And because of this, we can live daily in the Kingdom designed by Love Himself. Because of this, we are equipped to bring life and revival to a world that needs courage, boldness, and love.

And so, I ask you, are you ready? Are you ready for an adventure that can do as much to you as it can through you? Did you know that there is a place designed specifically for your heart, one that you can begin to experience today? Are you ready to step into who you are truly designed to be?

I hope you are, because He is ready for you and He has been for a long, long time.

> *Papa I pray that anyone who reads this book only hears Your words, not mine. I pray that You speak through these pages and that You will be glorified. I pray for an open mind to what You may have in store and that Your kingdom will be advanced. I pray that there is an outpouring of Your peace, rest, and love over all who encounters these pages. I pray favor into their lives and I pray rival for their hearts and for the world around them. Thank You for Your many blessings and thank You for Your continued work in our lives. Jesus come, rest in these pages and more importantly in anyone who is searching for You. Thank You Lord, You are so good.*

Chapter 2

HIS LOVE

Do you ever wonder what motivated Jesus to act?[1]

> Now a certain man was ill, Lazarus of Bethany, the village of Mary and her sister Martha. It was Mary who anointed the Lord with ointment and wiped his feet with her hair, whose brother Lazarus was ill. So the sisters sent to him, saying, "Lord, he whom you love is ill." But when Jesus heard it he said, "This illness does not lead to death. It is for the glory of God, so that the Son of God may be glorified through it."
>
> Now Jesus loved Martha and her sister and Lazarus. So, when he heard that Lazarus was ill, he stayed two days longer in the place where he was. Then after this he said to the disciples, "Let us go to Judea again."
>
> Then Jesus told them plainly, "Lazarus has died, and for your sake I am glad that I was not there, so that you may believe. But let us go to him." (John 11:1-4, 14)

When you read the rest of the story, you get to see Jesus speak tender truth, you get to experience Jesus feeling deep emotions, and you get to witness the healing power of our Lord as Lazarus is raised from the dead.[2] This is a triumphant tale, and yet why did Jesus postpone His departure to heal Lazarus? The name Lazarus means *God is my help*. But why was this help delayed?

Jesus wasn't worried He would fail, and He wasn't concerned about the persecution that He was experiencing in that region. Jesus says it was for our benefit that He waited. Jesus made the decision to wait two whole days before going to Lazarus, and this could not have been easy for Him since He weeps when He is among the mourners.[3] Jesus deeply cares for Lazarus, and yet He waits.

Jesus waited to go to Lazarus because the moment He would get to Lazarus, He was going to heal Him. Jesus can't help Himself. The moment that Jesus comes into contact with people who need healing, He heals them. If Jesus had gone to Lazarus when He got the news that Lazarus was ill, Jesus would have arrived and healed Lazarus from the sickness. This act of healing would have been good and pure, and people would have seen the power of God at work. But because Jesus waited two days, Lazarus was raised from the dead and we get to witness the greater miracle.

The amount of power it would have taken Jesus to heal Lazarus from the sickness is the same amount of power that it took Him to raise Lazarus from death. This is because it was the Spirit of God working through Him, not Jesus doing any sort of physical work. Because the power was the same despite waiting, Jesus chose to release a greater work into our midst.

And yet, this could not have been easy for Him. Jesus knows Lazarus and his sisters well, as we have several accounts of their interactions throughout Jesus's ministry. Jesus loves this family deeply. Jesus feels our emotions with us. He fully knew Lazarus would be raised from the dead, but that didn't stop the immediate sadness. That didn't take away the hurt and pain and loss that the people who loved Lazarus were feeling. Jesus knows the hope, and yet He feels the weight of emotion with the mourners. Jesus came to reveal to us the Father, and this tender moment tells us so much about the

Creator. He knows the triumphant ending—the grand crescendo He has designed for our victory—and yet He hurts with us today. What a tender and gracious God. He is the greatest Comforter.

There's another piece of this story that I love dearly. It happens before all the hustle and bustle and often goes unnoticed.

Mary and Martha know Jesus. The passage identifies Mary as the one who anointed Jesus and wiped His feet with her hair. They know Jesus intimately and have experienced His goodness and His power. They had looked into His eyes and seen His heart.

These sisters see that their brother is deeply sick and dying, and so they decide to send word to Jesus to get Him to help. This whole encounter is as much for their faith as it is for anyone else's. And they understand that they are asking a lot of Jesus, because the area He would be entering is extremely unsafe for Him. When Jesus said He was going to Lazarus, verse 16 says that one of the disciples remarks, "Let us also go, that we may die with him." This disciple isn't referring to Lazarus dying, but he was talking about Jesus dying. There was the very real possibility that Jesus was going to be caught and killed by the Jews if He went to Lazarus.

Now, if one of my sisters was dying and I was going to write to the Messiah to try to convince Him to help, I would take a lot of time and care to write that letter. I would list her credentials, her volunteer hours, and the number of mission trips she had been on. I would talk about how hard she works in school and about her previous growth and how much potential was still there. I would include references and notes and subscripts. I would also emphasize how much she loves Jesus.

But that is not the message Mary and Martha composed on behalf of their brother. These women have spent time with Jesus, and they must have asked themselves: What is it that is going to compel Jesus to come to Lazarus, despite the danger it would bring to Himself? What could they say to motivate Jesus to act?

And all they wrote was: "Lord, he whom you love is ill." They said, "The one You love is dying." They don't even give Lazarus's name, because the thing that compels Jesus to action the most is His love for us.

Mary and Martha saw their brother dying and knew how to respond. In the crisis, they knew Jesus well enough to know what to say. I want to sit so deeply at the Messiah's feet that when I get into a crisis or any struggle at all, I know immediately that Jesus will move simply because He loves me. This piece of His character is so beautiful and powerful. I truly believe we become unstoppable when we start to grasp what this can look like. We need to learn that it's about His love, not ever our actions or even our love for Him, that motivates Jesus to help us. And knowing His love transforms us in amazing ways.

> After saying these things, Jesus was troubled in his spirit, and testified, "Truly, truly, I say to you, one of you will betray me." The disciples looked at one another, uncertain of whom he spoke. One of his disciples, whom Jesus loved, was reclining at table at Jesus' side, so Simon Peter motioned to him to ask Jesus of whom he was speaking. So that disciple, leaning back against Jesus, said to him, "Lord, who is it?" (John 13:21-25)

Peter and John are two of the disciples, and Jesus loves them both dearly, just as He loves Lazarus. But there are some major differences between these two men. Both of them are incredible and go on to do extraordinary things for the Kingdom and are largely responsible for the church growing and developing. But in the above passage, John seems to know something that Peter hasn't grasped yet.

In the above passage, John is the disciple that is reclining with Jesus. This phrase means that he was lying on Jesus's chest. So basically, they are sitting around the table; and John is sitting next to Jesus, leaning on Him. Jesus is troubled and tells them that one will betray Him. Peter is across the table and jumps to action. He motions for John to ask who it is. Peter is trying to fix it. Peter is thinking, "If we know who it is, we can stop this. We can get ahead of this. Let's do something. Let's act." Peter's boldness led to a booming church later on, but at this moment, it is misplaced.

John asks the question, and Jesus answers. It's astonishing what Jesus tells them. Jesus answers our questions, even when the answer is hard to hear. Jesus loves Judas, too. He knows they will judge him, and He can probably tell Peter is ready to fight. But He tells them who it is because He trusts us with valuable information.

At this moment, Jesus has His last opportunity to talk with Judas, and He is calm and kind. He shows an example to His disciples even in a moment of total heart break that His love is yet greater. Jesus lets Judas walk out and expects the rest of the disciples to do the same. Jesus loved Judas until the very end, and maybe while watching Judas walk away, He was still holding out hope that Judas might come to know Love.

So, we have two opposing examples. In a moment of great trial, we have Peter trying to fix it and John who is leaning on Jesus, pressing in close to the heart of the Savior.

The name Peter means rock. Peter is an incredible apostle, is the first to name Jesus as the Christ, and is largely responsible for the creation of the church. But the name John means God is gracious. In this moment of betrayal, John leans into Jesus because he knows Love Himself. He knows what Grace looks like.

John is the only disciple that makes it to the foot of the cross. Peter is reportedly off crying because he denied Jesus.[4] Peter still finds redemption though. After he denies Jesus three times, the rooster crows not as a mark of his greatest sin but as the moment he was forgiven, because roosters crow in the morning. Jesus redeems Peter after the resurrection by asking him three times if he loves Him.[5] In this conversation, Jesus restores each moment of denial and weakness and helps Peter start the journey that led to the church we know today. Jesus pursues Peter's redemption and brings him to the foot of the cross so that Peter may know Grace.

But John was there when Jesus died, and John identifies himself as the one Jesus loves. John figured out first what we are fighting to know today. John saw the heart of the Father in Jesus, and He accepts the love fully. John knew that what motivates Jesus to act is His love, not ours. What would happen if we identified ourselves as the one Jesus loves? What could we accomplish if in the trials and troubles we lay our heads onto Jesus and know that He is Love and Grace? The entire earth groans for us to know this and step into it fully.

> For the creation waits in eager expectation for the children of God to be revealed. (Romans 8:19)

What could a world look like if we only ever called ourselves the one Jesus loves? To me, this is the only thing that I want to be called. For when I sin, which is often, I know that Love, Grace, and Truth are greater than I. So I choose daily to only ever be His love. Even in the heights of our sin, His heart is open for us to rest on Him, not because we are good, but because He is. It is always and forever about Him and His love for us.

You, dear child, are the one He loves.

> *Jesus, thank You for Your loving kindness. Thank You for Your goodness—for who You are. I ask that today and every day after, we only let one name stick to us. We are the ones You love. I pray that Your people may become free from anything that keeps them from this truth. I ask that You bring redemption to each one of us just as You did for Peter. Thank You for the ways You individually pursue our hearts and I ask that Your children will begin to be able to see the ways You relentlessly pursue them. I pray that Your Kingdom may be advanced as we learn Your love for us and that our response to You will bring You glory. You are so good and we love You.*

Chapter 3

RAGS TO RICHES

It's time for a little bit of Bible trivia. Please contain your excitement. Don't worry, it's only three questions and I'll give you the answers.

What is Abraham's wife's name? Sarah.

Abraham is the man chosen by God to become the father of nations. God changes his name from Abram, meaning high father, to Abraham, meaning father of a multitude, after making a covenant with him.[1] His wife receives a new name as well, going from Sarai, meaning princess, to Sarah, meaning mother of nations.[2]

Second question, what is Lot's wife's name? It's not a trick question. You don't know because her name is never given.[3]

Lot is Abraham's nephew.[4] Lot goes with Abraham when he left Egypt. Both of these men had a lot of belongings, such as livestock and tents, and so they needed a lot of land as they traveled together. They eventually decide to go different ways so that they wouldn't have to quarrel about space. Lot takes his belongings and moves to Sodom, a wicked and corrupt city.[5]

And the last question, what does Lot's wife turn into when she looks back onto the city of Sodom as it is being destroyed? She turns into salt.[6]

Sodom was a wicked city, and there came a point when God ordered it to be destroyed because the inhabitants wouldn't turn to

Him.[7] God sends two angels to retrieve Lot and his family in order to spare them from the impending destruction. As they flee, they are strictly instructed not to look back.[8] As Lot's wife looks upon the burning city, we see her heart.

Lot and his wife cared for Sodom, working to bring the people to God by relentless praying for the redemption of the city. When it was time to leave, Lot's wife couldn't let go. We keep our eyes fixed on what is most important to us, and Lot's wife's eyes were on the city where she labored. She found her value in the work she was doing, not the Creator she was doing it for.

Sarah wasn't perfect, but she was a daughter with great faith. She had her doubts about herself, laughing at God's promise that she would have a child because she was well past child-bearing age.[9] But her doubts never outweighed her heart for the Father. She followed God alongside her husband, with a pure heart and eyes only for the King. She believed the promises spoken over her, and because she had faith like her husband, Sarah and Abraham became parents of chosen generations. Every Christian today is a continuing fulfillment of God's promise to Abraham. Sarah receives a new name just like her husband. She is anointed and chosen because she never took her eyes off of the heavenly Father.

> Jesus said to him, "No one who puts his hand to plow and looks back is fit for the king-dom of God."(Luke 9:62)

Looking back is a matter of the heart. Lot's wife turned into salt when she looked back. Salt is not a bad thing. Jesus says we are the salt of the earth, but salt is useless when it is put onto the wrong things.[10] We are capable of doing extraordinary work, but if we fix our eyes on anything but the Lord, we are headed for disaster.

So often we fix our hearts onto things that aren't Him. We use work, our talents, or relationships to define us. We set worldly things before us and say Jesus is in there somewhere too. Jesus wants more than just part of us—He wants every piece of us.

I dated a guy my senior year in high school into my freshman year of college. We talked big talk and assumed that we were marriage-bound. When he asked for sex, I said yes. We broke up on our one year anniversary, which was during dead week of my first semester of college. That December was one of the hardest months of my life. I fell deeper into depression and cut the worst I ever have. I was broken because I had completely placed my worth in that relationship.

During the first week of January that next month, I went on a mission trip to Rio Bravo, Mexico; and Jesus was so sweet to my heart. He reminded me of His joy over me, and from that moment on, I have been chasing after Him with all my heart.

That next semester was filled with growth and healing like never before. Jesus pursued me as I pursued Him, and I healed tremendously as I walked with Him. Around February of that semester, there was going to be a college retreat at a ranch in Texas owned by Papa Joe and Fufi, the most amazing people I know. I love the ranch and of course signed up to go. A few weeks before the retreat, Fufi texted me and asked if I would be willing to dress up and take pictures around the ranch while I was there. They had recently started hosting weddings and needed pictures for advertising. I agreed because I love Fufi, but you should know that I hate pictures and I hate dressing up, except for on very rare occasions.

Dressing up in wedding dresses sounded kind of fun for a few seconds, and then I was struck that I myself did not deserve a white dress on my own wedding day. Up to that point in my healing, I had not yet talked with Jesus about my having sex; and now, I knew it was time to finally approach this subject. I prayed a lot leading up to this weekend and simply told Jesus that He was allowed to heal this area in my heart. I was nervous and scared of His disappointment, but I was ready to face it.

I was a little apprehensive about taking pictures, but the time finally arrived and us girls all went into to the room where the dresses were and started getting ready. I immediately picked a dress that was pitiful. It was old, ruffled, and yellow stained and had a large tear in the side. I put it on happily even though it was six inches too short. I was content with this pick and watched as the other two girls picked out their choice of skirts and dresses.

Fufi and her daughter Katie came into the room and began to inspect us to see if we were ready. With one look at me, they declared the dress I had picked wasn't good enough. I insisted it was perfectly fine, but they didn't agree. They looked through the other options until Fufi told Katie to get her wedding dress. Katie went and brought back the actual wedding dress she wore on her wedding day a few years before, and they made me put it on.

It was a perfect fit. Katie looked me over and almost cried because it was as if I was trying on dresses for my own wedding. Fufi found me a simple pearl necklace, and the look was complete. Papa Joe smiled in his special way, and I caught a glimpse of what my actual wedding day would be like. The afternoon was full of laughter and fun as we paraded around the ranch posing for pictures in the snow.

That weekend was perfect and will be a cherished memory for the rest of my life. At the time, I didn't realize the restoration process that I was walking in. But after some time, I sat and really thought about the day I had first put on a wedding dress and I saw what God had done for me. Without me even realizing it, He told me exactly what he thought of me. Without saying a word, He restored me into purity and forgave me fully.

When we set our hearts on things that aren't Him, when we fix our eyes on anything that isn't Jesus, and when we look back at our world and our old ways we compromise ourselves, we become nameless. Giving any part of our self to the world leaves us hurt, broken, and lost. We run into disaster if we aren't running to our Father.

Our God is good. He pursues our attention and affection and continually restores us to Himself. He takes the rags we wrap ourselves in and declares they are far from good enough. He clothes us in His righteousness and His love. He sets us apart for Himself as His bride and looks away from our iniquity. So often we hold tightly to our rags of mediocrity, sin, and shame and tell Him that it's okay. But He boldly declares over each of us, "Child, stop wearing those rags when I have designed you for My riches."

I fell into physical impurity because my heart became impure first. I held onto what that boy said about me as truth rather than having faith in what my Father was whispering over me all along. When the relationship ended, I crumbled because I had made it my identity; and without it, I was desperately looking around for something to define me. And Jesus came and scooped me up and told me that I was His. Since then, I have only ever listened to Him.

> By faith Sarah herself received power to conceive, even when she was past the age, since she considered Him faithful who had promised. (Hebrews 11:11)

Sarah had faith in what the Lord said to her over her doubts and fears. Lot's wife looked back because she found her worth in the work she was doing. Great faith is only possible when we fix our eyes on Jesus—the One who truly knows our worth. The cross is not a revelation of our sin; it is the definition of our worth.[11]

> The kingdom of heaven is like treasure hidden in a field, which a man found and covered up. Then in his joy he goes and sells all that he has and buys that field. (Matthew 13:44)

You are the treasure that Jesus found. You are the treasure He sold everything for. You are the treasure that He bought the entire surrounding field for your protection.[12]

You are bought at an extremely high price. Dare for a second to imagine what it cost to get you back. Heaven went bankrupt in the pursuit of you.[13] Your worth is predefined and not because of anything you did or could possibly do. Jesus says what you are worth, and to Him, you are worth suffering the single most painful death imaginable. Jesus suffered the complete separation from the Father so that we never have to.

Dare to believe what He says about you. Dare to declare over yourself today that you are a treasure. You are precious. You are loved by Love Himself. Dare to have faith despite the doubts, lies, and fears that surround you.

Sometimes we hold fast to our rags because we say, "This doesn't apply to me. How could He love me? After all that I've done? After all the time I spent away from Him?" We call ourselves misfits, sinners, dirty, tainted, stained, and unredeemable.

There was one day that I was driving around and jamming out to some of today's popular songs. Not the Christian popular songs, but secular tunes. And I sang along every explicit lyric, jamming out in my car, and just having fun. I had a moment where the next song I was going to play was a Christian one, but I stopped myself. I was thinking that I would wait until I got home to listen to a worship song since Jesus probably didn't want me praising Him the second I got done swearing. In that moment, very clearly, Jesus declared to me, "I did not suffer the most painful death possible to spend one more second away from you."

Maybe we need to stop telling Jesus what He thinks and listen to what He says.

> *Jesus, thank You for what You have done for us. Thank You for what You say about us. Help us to look only at You. Strip our hearts down until the only thing we long for is more of You. May we never look back to the world. Give us the boldness and courage to only ever look forward to You. Give us the strength we need today to finally believe what You say about us. Purify our hearts Papa. Increase our faith so that we may know You better. Thank You for Your kindness and gentleness and patience. You are a good Father. Take away anything that hinders us from knowing Your heart over us. Thank You Jesus. Thank You for taking our place. Thank You for transforming us from rags to riches.*

Chapter 4

ORPHANS NO MORE

Throughout the Bible, we are called children of God. When teaching the disciples to pray, Jesus instructs them to approach God as our Father in heaven, and it's the same for us. The significance of this should not be lost. He longs for us to know Him as our Father.

In Biblical times, the family was central to life. Every part of yourself and your life revolved around your family. You lived on your family's property for your entire life, only leaving if you were a woman marrying into a different family.

The families were ruled by the oldest male. This man was in charge of the entire household, and his name gave definition to each member of the family.

In this culture, the firstborn son was special. He received most of the inheritance and all of the responsibility. He would work, train, and learn directly from the father. This son was groomed from his birth to one day step into the leading role. It was imperative for him to learn under his father so that he would be able to make the family prosper for further generations.

Any other sons would receive minimal inheritance in comparison to the oldest brother. They would be responsible for laboring for the family and estate. These men would work for their household for their entire life, never leaving home. If they took a wife, she would become a part of the husband's family and join him on his established property.

Women of the family received no inheritance. They were responsible for the chores including cooking, cleaning, raising the children, and making sure the house was in order for the men. Women were completely defined by the man over her household. Daughters were able to marry into a different family only if it was arranged by the head of her household.

If the man of a household was to die and there were no men in the family to step into the leading role, the women would receive none of the inheritance or estate that was remaining. The women would become undefined and nameless. They would lose what they once had and would have no means of getting what they needed, including food and shelter. They would have no hope because very rarely would another man step in and take responsibility for the women. They became orphans.

Left with very few options for survival, some of these women would prostitute themselves to get by. A once honored and respected woman could very quickly become shameful and despised as she desperately tried to get food and shelter. Forced to resort to prostitution, a woman would become an orphan in her society without any hope of a better future.[1]

It's very good news to us that God Himself has a family household. In God's family, He has one Son. Jesus receives the entirety of God's inheritance because He is the first and only Son. This means that everything our God has, every single piece, belongs to Jesus. And this delights our God! He enjoys giving Jesus what is His. He loves bestowing onto His Son the entirety of His household inheritance.

We live as orphans in this world. We are the nameless woman without a household. We are all prostitutes, selling ourselves for survival because we live in a fallen world. Death and destruction are all around, for we are lost and abandoned as we try to survive in a world we don't belong to. We are dead in our sin.[2] But we do not stay this way.

The Heavenly Father knew we would become orphans, and so He put into action a rescue plan. He was not obligated to act, but He did the unthinkable to redeem us to Himself. God always wanted us to be a part of His family, and so He makes that very thing possible through Jesus Christ.

> While he was still speaking to the people, behold, his mother and his brothers stood outside, asking to speak to him. But he replied to the man who told him, "Who is my mother, and who are my brothers?" And stretching out his hand toward his disciples, he said, "Here are my mother and my brothers! For whoever does the will of my Father in heaven is my brother and sister and mother." (Matthew 12:46–50)

Sitting in that room were the apostles and disciples from all around—men and women who had been following Jesus, listening to His instructions, and daring to believe that this was the promised Messiah. Imagine Jesus's great pleasure in being able to declare to the orphans before Him that they had a new household. Think about the grin on Jesus's face as He declared boldly that those following Him were orphans no more.

Jesus's words would have been met with large confusion. The crowd before Him knew that one couldn't simply become a part of a different household. And yet Jesus was calling the people around Him his brothers and sisters.

God declares that we are His and His alone. He sent His only Son to atone for our sins and to make it possible for us to enter His household. He gives us a new name and joyfully blesses us with an inheritance. Not only are we forgiven, but also we are adopted into the most powerful family in existence. Our adoption is signed and sealed in blood. The act is done—You are a child of God.

Adoption is beautiful and pure, but not necessarily easy. There are two parties involved who face very different journeys. The parents know beforehand that they want the child, and they dive headfirst into doing whatever it takes to get this child home. The parents must fight to make it happen. Today, there's a lot of paperwork, time, and money involved in the process. For God, it took the death of His Son.

Parents must pick up arms and go to battle to get their child. Meanwhile, the child is unaware of what is happening for them. They have no idea their life is going to change. They trudge forward, orphans without a reason to hope, not knowing that there is a war going on for them. They do nothing to aid the process. The children of adoption don't fight the battle—They experience the rescue.

This is what our Father did for us. He waged war for our lives and won outright. He gives us a hope, an inheritance, a legacy, and a name. God intervened for us and adopted us into His household long before we knew we even needed a new life.

Dear child of God, do not let the significance of this be lost. You are an orphan to this world because you have been adopted by your Father who is in heaven. This world has nothing for you because your Father has given everything to you.

Papa, may we know the significance of these things. May we rediscover our adoption. May we abandon the world that betrays us and know only what it means to be in Your household forevermore. Help us to digest these truths so that we may be forever changed. Help us to find the faith to declare these truths boldly into our lives as well as the lives of the people around us. Thank You for adopting us. Thank You for rescuing us and giving us new names. Thank You for Your inheritance. May we learn to live in the fullness of being Your sons and daughter.

Sweetly Broken

Chapter 5

JARS OF CLAY

The thief comes only to steal and kill and destroy. I came that they may have life and have it abundantly. (John 10:10)

You are the "they" that Jesus is talking about here. An abundant life does not include a broken heart. Jesus cares about your healing. Your Father wants you to be healed and whole so that you can live in the freedom Jesus bought for you.

But he was pierced for our transgressions; he was crushed for our iniquities; upon him was the chastisement that brought us peace, and with his wounds we are healed. (Isaiah 53:5)

He himself bore our sins in his body on the tree, that we might die to sin and live to righteousness. By his wounds you have been healed. (1 Peter 2:24)

A different version says, "By His stripes you are healed." Jesus was striped when He was whipped. The cross was enough to satisfy sin, so His whipping was not necessary to defeat death. Jesus took the whipping for our healing, making Jesus the Healer.

Jesus knows how you have been hurt. He sees your scars, your pain, and your battle wounds. You may be able to hide your pain from friends, family, and even yourself; but you aren't fooling Him. Jesus took your healing into His hands. You are healed. What you need now is truth that can come in and replace the lies that keep you from walking in the fullness of life.

Jesus longs to work deeper into our hearts. He gently knocks on the doors we have shut off within ourselves. He respects us when we don't let Him in, but He keeps knocking. Our Healer is a gentleman, and He only knocks on doors when He knows we are ready to tackle whatever is behind them.

In the following chapters, I want to equip you with tools that I have used to navigate my own healing. Jesus longs to speak to your heart individually, and I encourage you to adapt what you read to fit you best. But to allow the Lord to work, there are a few things that you have to be willing to do. You have to be willing to be vulnerable. You have to be honest with yourself, God, and others. You have to be willing to let Him into whatever area of yourself He is asking to go.

This journey will look different for every person. Don't spend a single second looking around you to see what other people are experiencing. Put your eyes fully on Jesus, and you will be healed.

And know that there is nothing wrong with being broken.

> For God, who said, "Let light shine out of darkness," has shone in our hearts to give the light of the knowledge of the glory of God in the face of Jesus Christ. But we have this treasure in jars of clay, to show that the surpassing power belongs to God and not to us. (2 Corinthians 4:6–7)

The light of God revealed in Christ has been placed in our hearts. This light needs to be seen. People need to know who our Father is. The Lord put this light into something extremely fragile—

not only breakable and thin but also beautiful and intricate, like jars of clay that need to be crafted with care. They need individual attention and tender treatment. We are these jars of clay that the Father so wonderfully crafted.

But who puts the light of the world and the most important message into something so feeble and weak? No one sensible, no one logical, but yet our God did. He placed the most important knowledge into vessels that would need the care of the most skilled Potter.

But how are people to see a light that is in a jar? There has to be cracks, holes, or rifts. There need to be gaps and fissures throughout the clay so that the light within can shine into the darkness surrounding it. For this world to know our King, we must be open and honest with our brokenness so that the world may see the surpassing power of the one true God. This is terrifying, but you can do it because He is with you. "Take heart," Jesus says, "for I have overcome the world."[1]

Vulnerability enables deeper community. If you open yourself up to the Father, you will very quickly find yourself in a deeply intimate relationship with Him. And nothing is sweeter than that. Abba will only ever greet you with tender love and affection. He does not use guilt, shame, or condemnation to fix us. He uses love, truth, and conviction to help us. And like the Bible itself, this journey starts with a garden.

Father, prepare us for Your healing touch. May every person who reads this book learn something new about You and about themselves. Papa, teach us how beautiful our individual story is and help us to not shy away from Your touch. Be gentle, tender, and kind to us. Please only go where we are ready, Father. I ask boldly that the following tools stay pure and completely under Your guidance. I declare boldly that this information may not be twisted or tainted away from Your truths. I ask that Your hands be strongly involved in the following chapters and that each person reading may become equipped

to heal in the way that they need. Thank You for
Your strength and Your Holy Spirit. Thank You for
Your love for us Papa, and may we come to know
Your love more each and every day.

Chapter 6

ROOTS AND FRUITS

Beware of false prophets, who come to you in sheep's clothing but inwardly are ravenous wolves. You will recognize them by their fruits. Are grapes gathered from thornbushes, or figs from thistles? So, every healthy tree bears good fruit, but the diseased tree bears bad fruit. A healthy tree cannot bear bad fruit, nor can a diseased tree bear good fruit. Every tree that does not bear good fruit is cut down and thrown into the fire. Thus you will recognize them by their fruits." (Matthew 7:15–20)

Despite the fact that I had to take a plant and soil science class in college, I don't know very much about plants. But there is one thing I do know that is a universal fact for every single plant that grows on this earth. If the roots are bad, the fruits are bad. This is logical though because the roots are the source that the fruits are growing from. If the roots are dying, sick, or not getting needed nutrients, how could the fruit possibly be any good? In other words, what we abide in determines what we grow into.

There is a very direct relationship between roots and fruits. The roots are the cause of the fruits. Never does changing the fruit have any effect on the roots. Only by changing the roots can there be any hope of change in the fruits. Fruits can't lie. Fruits expose the state of the root.

This is often true within ourselves. The fruits we bear are a reflection of the roots we are keeping. Whatever we root our heart into is what we grow from. We see the fruits we are bearing, and sometimes we just try to make the fruit better. We resolve to stop lying and work hard to watch what we say. We resolve to be better humans and try to force ourselves to love the people around us. We look at the bad fruit and think, "If I can just do this list of things or stop doing these other things, everything will be fine."

There are deeper roots that need our attention. A lot of the bad fruit we bear can be transformed by digging our roots deeper in Jesus. Living full heartedly for Him changes a lot of things about us without us even trying to change. But sometimes roots need more than just a little tugging. Sometimes, we need to learn why we do certain things to stop believing lies and be enabled to run fully after Jesus.

For example, I used to cut. I knew it wasn't right and I would tell myself that I wasn't going to do it again, but then things happened and I would find myself cutting once more. In my second semester of college, I started to run whole heartedly after Jesus. We got to talking one day, and I started to think about the times I would want to cut. What I desired most when I cut was human attention. I wanted someone to notice me—to say that they saw my pain and that they could help me. I was longing for genuine attention. The day I admitted this to myself and to Jesus, He told me that His eyes never left me. Jesus told me that I was always on His mind and He was always right there, paying attention to me. Now, whenever I feel like I may be overlooked, I just remind myself that the Creator desires to play an active role in my life and that I always have His undivided attention. And without trying to stop cutting, it is no longer even a thought of mine. I know I will never again cut myself to get worldly attention.

Roots are scary. Roots dig deep into ourselves and often force honesty and vulnerability. Roots very often result from lies, fears, and hurts that we have been carrying around for a long time. But we need to dig deep and make room for healthy roots to begin to grow so that Jesus can have His way in us. We need only one root system, and we will be sustained and healthy for our entire lives. We need strong and deep roots in Jesus.

We can't grow what hasn't been cultivated. Jesus is an excellent gardener, and He knows just how to prune us so that we can walk with Him fully. We need to abide completely in Him if we want any good fruit.

> I am the true vine, and my Father is the vinedresser. Every branch in me that does not bear fruit he takes away, and every branch that does bear fruit he prunes, that it may bear more fruit. Already you are clean because of the word that I have spoken to you. Abide in me, and I in you. As the branch cannot bear fruit by itself, unless it abides in the vine, neither can you, unless you abide in me. I am the vine; you are the branches. Whoever abides in me and I in him, he it is that bears much fruit, for apart from me you can do nothing. If anyone does not abide in me he is thrown away like a branch and withers; and the branches are gathered, thrown into the fire, and burned. If you abide in me, and my words abide in you, ask whatever you wish, and it will be done for you. By this my Father is glorified, that you bear much fruit and so prove to be my disciples. As the Father has loved me, so have I loved you. Abide in my love. If you keep my commandments, you will abide in my love, just as I have kept my Father's commandments and abide in His love. These things I have spoken to you, that my joy may be in you, and that your joy may be full. (John 15:1–11)

We all desire to produce good fruits, but we can't grow good fruits just by wanting to see those fruits. We all have heard of the fruit of the Spirit—love, joy, peace, patience, kindness, goodness, faithfulness, gentleness, and self-control.[1] When you look at the word love that is used here, part of the definition in Greek specifies that it is only produced by the Spirit. This means that it is not us that are doing these things, but the Spirit working through us. These characteristics will be so distinct to the Spirit, and they will just naturally flow through us when we abide in Him.

Fruit will grow. The only way to affect what kind of fruit you produce is through the roots. Abide in Jesus, rest in Him, and you will see good fruit.

> *Jesus, take us to our roots. If anything deep in us is not of You, we ask that you remove it. We want to be people living whole heartedly for You. Prune us so that we can know Your love more fully. Thank You for being the True Vine. Thank You for grafting us into You. Teach us how to abide completely in You Jesus.*

Chapter 7

THE STILL SMALL VOICE

Have you ever thought about how we assume that a deaf person can't speak? In reality, they are able to learn high-functioning speech patterns because their vocal chords are intact. The added challenge is learning to pronounce words without being able to hear them or to hear the sound of their own voice.

When you can't hear, you don't know what words sound like. Learning to speak comes from hearing how things are pronounced. When we speak, we are mimicking what we have heard.

If we are deaf to the voice of the Father, we won't be able to speak what He is saying. You can't speak what you don't hear. The word of God is living and active, and we get the opportunity to speak the things He is whispering. We need to know His voice. We can't rely on just taking what other people proclaim that He has said. We need to be hearing from Him ourselves.

Know that God wants to talk to you. He has given us the ability to speak directly to Him. We aren't playing a massive game of telephone where the words of God are being passed from person to person to person, finally reaching us, distorted and misquoted. We have been given a direct connection to the King. We get to hear His words firsthand, straight from Him.

We need to know His voice. We will always be learning and growing in our understanding of Him. Maybe you've tried talking to Him but felt like you weren't getting anything back or maybe you've talked and didn't realize He was talking back. I want to offer you a few tips to help you begin to dig deeper into knowing His voice.

God is extremely personal. The way one person hears Him may not be the way you do. He longs to speak to us as individuals, and He will connect to you on a deeply personal level. He knows your heart for He created it. You don't have to go looking for Him in new and far-off places. He wants to speak to you today, right where you are. He loves to tell us things through what we love, and He wants to bless us in ways special to our hearts.

God will never contradict Himself. If you think you hear something but aren't sure, check it with scripture. Dig deep into the Word to help you learn His desires. The Bible is the most important tool in learning who He is and what He is saying. Knowing His character is central to knowing His voice. If you are having trouble on even beginning to know what He is saying, scripture is a good place to start. Read the things Jesus said and know that He is speaking them to you today.

Community is another important tool in learning His voice. As a group of people desiring to know Him, we can encourage and strengthen one another as we learn what He is saying. If you think that you hear Him saying something but you aren't sure or want to double-check, talk to someone trustworthy who is walking in the Holy Spirit and ask them to pray into it with you. Jesus wants to confirm to us that we know His voice and will very often speak to us through other people.

Sometimes we just assume that every thought we have is from us. Being aware that God is speaking to you can help you start to discern when it may be Him speaking. He may not use words directly either. He can communicate through pictures, feelings, the words of other people, and perceiving things, like when you just know something but no one told you and you can't explain how you know. There are endless ways that the Father can speak to us, and it is important that if you think He is speaking, you stop and listen. We are created to know His words and sense His Spirit. If you feel like it is Him, you could very well be right.

Ask Him questions. He is a Teacher and a Father; He loves our curiosity. Sometimes when I present a question to Him, I sit and repeat the same question a few times as I listen. Not because I think He's not answering, but because I am quieting my mind to be able to hear Him more clearly.

> How amazing are your thoughts concerning me, God! How vast is the sum of them! Were I to count them, they would outnumber the grains of sand. (Psalm 139:17–18)

God has a lot of thoughts about you, so start to ask Him what a few of them are. He longs to tell you His heart for you. Ask Him, and He will answer.

Sometimes we have questions that we are timid to tell God. There is nothing wrong with having doubt, but we need to bring them to Jesus instead of hiding in fear.

> Now Thomas, one of the Twelve, called the Twin, was not with them when Jesus came. So the other disciples told him, "We have seen the Lord." But he said to them, "unless I see in his hands the mark of the nails, and place my finger into the mark of the nails, and place my hand into his side, I will never believe."
> Eight days later, his disciples were inside again, and Thomas was with them. Although the doors were locked, Jesus came and stood among them and said, "Peace be with you." Then he said to Thomas, "Put your finger here, and see my hands; and put out your hand, and place it in my side. Do not disbelieve, but believe." Thomas answered him, "My Lord and my God!" (John 20:24–28)

Thomas was having doubts that Jesus had actually risen from the grave. And Jesus marches right up to him, despite the locked door, and helps him to see. Jesus wants to come through for you. He doesn't shy away from hard questions. Tell Him your doubts and let Him show you His goodness and power.

One of my favorite things about the Bible is that it is the only book that the author will never die. He longs to tell you more about His Word. Ask Him for deeper insight. Ask Him to make the words come alive. Ask Him for a new hunger to dig into what is written in those pages.

Sometimes as we read the Bible, things can seem harsh. Some of the things Jesus says can easily sound mean. But the people He says them to respond differently, which tells me that we are reading it with the wrong tone. We all read the Bible and view life through lenses. These lenses hinder us from knowing what God is saying, or they cause us to hear it in the wrong tone. Ask God if He would remove the lenses you wear. Ask Him for new eyes to encounter His word and see His character as He truly is.[1]

Sometimes we have placed walls and barriers around ourselves. We can feel a fog or a distance or just feel like we aren't getting anywhere. Breakthrough is hindered because we have parts of our self tightly guarded. Ask Jesus to tell you where the wall is. Ask Him what it's surrounding. And when you're ready, ask Him to tear it down or to help you tear it down. Our Father longs to break down everything that separates us from Him. If you can't even name what is holding you back, just ask Him to come in and tear it all down.[2]

Sometimes we have bad memories that we can still remember today—those painful moments that we felt alone and hurt and helpless. Sometimes we can't even imagine what could possibly make those haunting memories go away or get any better. But Jesus wants to flood even the most painful moments and show you how He was there for you. Ask Him where He was. Ask Him how He was there for you even in the worst of times. He will comfort you today from the hurts of yesterday. By letting Jesus show us where He was in those times, we are better able to heal from them. Finding Jesus in the pains of the past can release us to chase Him more fully in the present.[3]

Ask Jesus to show you what lies you believe. And as soon as He tells you, ask Him to replace the lie with His truth. Fill your mind with only the things He speaks over you.

There is one more tool that is extremely important. It is a central part of the Good News of the Gospel, and it is vital for any sort of personal growth. We need Jesus to renew our minds, and we need to repent.

> Repent, for the Kingdom of Heaven has come near. (Matthew 3:2)

We will be coming back to this verse, but for right now, we are just going to talk about that first word. Repent means to change the way you think. We need to shift our thoughts away from the worldly perspective we have and ask Jesus to tell us how He thinks. We need heavenly vision to be able to accomplish what we are called to do on this earth. Ask Jesus how He wants you to think about the different aspects of your life—jobs, money, worries, doubts, fears, people, family, friends, anything, and everything. So often, we get bogged down in areas that Jesus has already shown us the example of how to live. By repenting, we enable the Father to come in and replace lies with powerful truths.

> *Jesus, thank You for always speaking to us. We rejoice that Your Word is alive and active! Teach us to know Your voice. Speak loudly and boldly to us. Answer our questions; increase our faith. Lead us into deeper relationship with You as we learn to talk directly with You. Thank You for being personal to our hearts. Thank You for answering us, and teaching us, and walking with us.*

Chapter 8

POWERFUL WORDS

I'm going to tell you something that took me a very long time to figure out. The devil is a liar. He's probably lying to you right now. But we can gloriously hope because truth will always be more powerful than any lie.

> So Jesus said to the Jews who had believed him, "If you abide in my word, you are truly my disciples, and you will know the truth, and the truth will set you free." (John 8:31–32)

Truth can flood any lie that may be holding you back. If you don't think that there is any lie about yourself that you may be believing, you are most likely mistaken. We are precious and valuable to the King, and because of this, we are targeted by the enemy to try to keep us from Abba. But the thing is, the enemy has no real power over you; he can only suggest lies that you then get to choose to believe or not.

For a long time, I hated myself. Throughout middle school and most of high school, I genuinely did not like myself. I believed that everyone's life would be better if I simply didn't exist, and I often day dreamed of ways that I could be removed from life. I was wrapped in these lies, until one day when I was studying Daniel.

King Belshazzar made a great feast for a thousand of his lords and drank wine in front of the thousand. Belshazzar, when he tasted the wine, commanded that the vessels of gold and of silver that Nebuchadnezzar his father had taken out of the temple in Jerusalem be brought, that the king and his lords, his wives, and his concubines might drink from them. Then they brought in the golden vessels that had been taken out of the temple, the house of God in Jerusalem, and the king and his lords, his wives, and his concubines drank from them. They drank wine and praised the gods of gold and silver, bronze, iron, wood, and stone. (Daniel 5:1–4)

Right after this is the handwriting on the wall that Daniel interprets as the doom of King Belshazzar. But what is happening in this passage is extremely significant. In order to show off to his subjects and because he was proud, Belshazzar used cups taken from the temple to serve wine at a party. They used holy vessels for unholy activity. They were laughing at God and defiling what had been made holy for Him. They were treating the holy as if it was common. And the enemy still does this today.

God has sealed us to Himself. Nothing, not even God, can remove this seal. But we can be convinced that we aren't sealed. We are holy vessels, but we are being treated as if we were common. The enemy ravishes in lying to us, making us think we are not holy.

You are holy and sealed by the Lord, nothing can make this untrue, but the enemy loves to treat the holy as common. The devil lies to us, doing whatever he can to convince us that we aren't holy. The only power Satan has is the power we give him when we believe any lie that he tells us.

There are other voices besides our Father that are talking to us. We will face spiritual warfare, and it is dangerous not to be conscious of it. There are lies all around us that are trying to do whatever it takes to keep us from knowing our true identity.

Learning that I believed lies didn't instantly heal me of all hurts, but it did break the chains that were on me and allow me to run after truth. We fight lies with truth. Truth is more powerful than any lie will ever be. Know what the Father is saying over you. Learn to distinguish what His truths are for you so that when the lies try to get in, you have already defeated them. Light always beats darkness.

Whenever light shines, darkness has to leave. It's not that darkness leaves—It just stops. Darkness is the absence of light, and so when light appears, the darkness simply stops existing. This is why bringing things into the light is so powerful. Whenever we speak out lies or fears or struggles, the enemy's power over those things disappears, and Papa's truth has the opportunity to flood in. When we keep things in the dark, we are living in fear. But when we speak out of the darkness, we trust fully that light will come rushing in. Speaking things out is powerful because words are powerful.

Our words are powerful because His words are powerful. The things we speak often reflect how we feel on the inside, and they can affect the realities around us. Our words have the power to bring life, but they also have the power to destroy, which is why the Bible tells us that the tongue needs taming.

The Bible talks a lot about forgiveness. Forgiveness is extremely powerful, and Jesus teaches on it often.

> For if you forgive others their trespasses,
> your heavenly Father will also forgive you, but
> if you do not forgive others their trespasses,
> neither will your Father forgive your trespasses.
> (Matthew 6:14–15)

The state of forgiveness is love. Forgiveness is a decision, not an emotion. You can forgive someone while still feeling hurt, broken, or sad. Choosing forgiveness means we are choosing to love rather than hate. When we forgive, our heart is set up in prime position for our Father to work in us. God can do impressive things with a heart that is attached to His. When we forgive, we open ourselves up to experience our Father's love in deeper realms.

Jesus died for the forgiveness of all sins. If you don't believe this, you don't yet know the work of the cross. Jesus has already forgiven all offenses—the ones done by us, the ones directed at us, and even all those directed at Him. Jesus already chose forgiveness. Holding out on forgiveness for someone works directly against the cross.

The only person your unforgiveness effects is you. Your offender has already been forgiven. Not choosing forgiveness keeps you outside of the Kingdom.

Sometimes we don't offer forgiveness because we refuse to acknowledge the hurt. When we do this, we aren't trusting that the grace of Jesus is enough for them. All sin is forgiven; grace is enough. It is okay to admit that you have been hurt by the people you care about. Acknowledge the pain and allow Jesus's grace and forgiveness to do its works.

We must constantly choose forgiveness. We match Christ's heart when we are quick to forgive. Be in the practice of offering complete and instant forgiveness because you yourself have constant and complete forgiveness. Forgiveness enables us to have deeper connects with the people in our lives as well as with our Lord. Forgiveness keeps us humble and positions our heart to dwell in a place where the Father is able to move within us as He pleases.

Community is important, and we need to call out the light in the people around us. We need to be encouraging and kind to the people we interact with daily. Having good community to encourage us is a huge blessing. But we need to join the fight over ourselves as well. We need to be speaking good things into our own lives. We cannot be sustained solely on the praise of others. Learning to speak only good things over ourselves can be weird and challenging, but we need to align our thoughts for ourselves with the thoughts the Father has for us.

The words Jesus has for you are good and kind. Abide in Him and choose to only believe the things He declares over you. And He declares nothing but good things!

Jesus, thank You for giving us the power to speak life. Thank You for forgiving us and making us holy. Jesus, take away all the lies that are keeping us from knowing Your heart. Break any chain that binds us. Help us know that we are sealed. Give us a new revelation today of the things You say over us. May we be bold people who refuse to believe any lie that comes our way. Help us know when we are experiencing warfare, and remind us that You fight on our behalf. Keep us under Your protection, and may we never allow a lie to affect us again.

Chapter 9

THE STORM

And when he [Jesus] got into the boat, his disciples followed him. And behold, there arose a great storm on the sea, so that the boat was being swamped by the waves; but he was asleep. And they went and woke him, saying, "Save us, Lord; we are perishing." And he said to them, "Why are you afraid, O you of little faith?" Then he rose and rebuked the winds and the sea, and there was a great calm. And the men marveled, saying, "What sort of man is this, that even winds and sea obey him?" (Matthew 8:23–27)

On that day, when evening had come, he [Jesus] said to them, "Let us go across to the other side." And leaving the crowd, they took him with them in the boat, just as he was. And other boats were with him. And a great windstorm arose, and the waves were breaking into the boat, so that the boat was already filling. But he was in the stern, asleep on the cushion. And they woke him and said to him, "Teacher, do you not care that we are perishing?" And he awoke and rebuked the wind and said to the sea, "Peace! Be still!" And the wind ceased, and there was a great calm. He said to them, "Why are you so afraid? Have you still no faith?" And they were filled with great fear and said to one another, "Who then is this, that even the wind and the sea obey him?" (Mark 4:35–41)

One day he [Jesus] got into a boat with his disciples, and he said to them, "Let us go across to the other side of the lake." So they set out, and as they sailed he fell asleep. And a windstorm came down on the lake, and they were filling with water and were in danger. And they went and woke him, saying, "Master, Master, we are perishing!" And he awoke and rebuked the wind and the raging waves, and they ceased, and there was a calm. He said to them, "Where is your faith?" And they were afraid, and they marveled, saying to one another, "Who then is this, that he commands even winds and water, and they obey him?" (Luke 8:22–25)

Let's go back to this day in history and really imagine what this moment was like. If you would go with me, back to this boat.

Jesus and the 12 disciples have been traveling together for a little while now. Masses have come to hear Jesus teach a radical new way of thinking, and His disciples are trying to figure everything out. They love Jesus and enjoy His company, but it hasn't become fully known to them yet that Jesus is the Messiah.

They get onto this boat and set sail to the other side of the lake. As they sail, the waves start to crash a little, and the wind picks up; but no one is worried. Most of the disciples were professional fishermen, so a bit of rough sea would have been nothing.

As they continue on, the waves and wind begin to increase, and the storm arrives. The men laugh together and continue sailing.

As the storm continues to set in, the sailors begin to brag about the storms they have sailed through. The boasts and brags go on until slowly some of the less experienced start to get nervous. The storm continues to worsen, and tension starts to rise.

The nonsailors and least experienced start to get really nervous now as the storm is rising in intensity. Still, the most confident ones smile. But there is tension in their foreheads as they begin to fear what will happen if it gets any worse.

And the storm worsens. The wind howls, and the waves beat the sides of the boat as they are pushed this way and that. Now even the biggest bragger has begun to panic. Water fills the boat and men get to work bailing out what they can, but still the waterline rises. It becomes clear that there will be no break, no rest, or no peace. The sailors know what this means. They know that no one has survived sailing through a storm of this size.

The men look at one another and see dead men, waiting for their doom. Their lives are forfeit unless something changes. There was no getting out of this storm.

The men begin to say their goodbyes. Some pass on last words. Someone decides to go tell Jesus that they are dying. They didn't expect Him to do anything; they just wanted Him to know that it was over—They were perishing. The storm had bested them and their lives were over.

But Jesus comes onto the deck, and something's different. The air buzzes as Jesus walks to the edge of the boat and looks out onto the sea. The disciples wonder what could possibly be happening. Quietly, gently, Jesus whispers, "Be still."

And the waves stop.

And the winds cease.

And the storm is over. Done. With a word, it is finished.

The men don't know what to do. They stop and can't comprehend what has just happened. Some hug, while some giggle in relief. Slowly, a wave of peace runs throughout every person on the boat.

They realize that there is still water in the boat. All men grab buckets as they work to bail out every last drop of water that got into the boat during the storm.

As they work, they marvel at the man named Jesus. They wonder who this man could be in that the wrath of nature would obey Him. But they rejoice, for they were dead men on a sinking ship, and now they are alive!

And this is us. This is our salvation story. We were dead on a sinking ship—Until Jesus stepped in and did what we couldn't. Jesus defeated death and will be back one day to destroy it for good.

Jesus saved us—We are saved. But there is some contaminant that lingers behind from the storm. The water that filled the boat didn't all fall out when the storm stopped. We bail out the water through the renewal of our mind and repentance.

> As obedient children, do not be conformed
> to the passions of your former ignorance, but as
> he who called you is holy, you also be holy in all
> your conduct, since it is written, "You shall be
> holy, for I am holy." (1 Peter 1:14–16)

Jesus declares bold things over us; it's time we boldly declare with Him. If He says you are saved, then you are saved. If He says you are healed, then you are healed. If He says you are pure, then you are pure. If He says you are righteous, then you are righteous. If He says you are holy, then you are holy.

The storm is the story of our salvation—our righteousness, our healing, our purity, and our holiness. Jesus came and calmed every storm that we may find ourselves in. He declares good things over us, and it is time that we join in agreement and declare with Him.

The water that's still in the boat does not take away from the fact that the storm is over. You were dead; now you are alive. We continue to repent and renew our minds as a testament to the fact that Jesus has saved us.

Trying to continue sailing as if there is still a storm gets us nowhere. Jesus already saved us; Jesus calmed the storm. Now, we get to listen to what He has to say and believe Him. Don't be a "O ye, of little faith." Be bold in your faith of who Jesus is. Believe what He says about you. Join Him in the rest and peace of your salvation, and continually renew your mind so that you may know Him and His love more.

Jesus, thank You for saving us. Thank You for stopping the storm that we could never have survived on our own. Remind us daily of who You are. Help us find the courage and strength to believe all that You say. Renew our minds today Lord, show us the ways that we need to repent, and may we always be looking for ways to better align our thoughts with Yours.

Chapter 10

THE NAME OF GOD

When we heal the image we have of God, we heal within ourselves.[1] Our God is perfect and good, but a lot of times, we project what we see on this fallen earth as having to do with His character. When we are given revelation of who He really is, many things in our hearts align back to our original design.

As you study Scripture, you will find that God has many names. Each one reveals specific and unique things about His immeasurable character. I would like to point out three names that are often not necessarily considered names.

God is Love. Jesus is Grace. The Holy Spirit is Truth.

As I have read Scripture, I find seeing these words seen as names can magnify the passages they are in. These names help identify the character of each Godhead and help us grow in our understanding of them. You need love, you know Love. You need grace, you know Grace. You need truth, you know Truth.

Our God is three in One, which is understood yet not understood. It is confusing, and I don't think we are able to fully understand the depths of the Trinity. But we do know that the Trinity is the Father, Son, and Holy Spirit. We know that all three are God. We oftentimes connect with One of the Three more than the others. Oftentimes, the Holy Spirit may seem scary or the Father may seem distant or Jesus may seem uninterested. Something so beautiful about the three entities is that we can connect with each in different ways, but we must always remember that they are the same God.

> Long ago, at many times and in many ways, God spoke to our fathers by the prophets, but in these last days he has spoken to us by his Son, whom he appointed the heir of all things, through whom also he created the world. He is the radiance of the glory of God and the exact imprint of his nature, and he upholds the universe by the word of his power. After making purification for sins, he sat down at the right hand of the Majesty on high, having become as much superior to angels as the name he has inherited is more excellent than theirs. (Hebrews 1:1–4)

This description of Jesus is extremely powerful, but there's one aspect I want to highlight. Jesus is the "exact imprint" of God. Jesus came to earth to reveal the Father to us, and Jesus is the exact same as the Father.

> If you love me, you will keep my commandments. And I will ask the Father, and he will give you another Helper, to be with you forever, even the Spirit of truth, whom the world cannot receive, because it neither sees him nor knows him. You know him, for he dwells with you and will be in you. (John 14:15–17)

The word "another" in this passage roughly means "the exact same."[2] Jesus is saying that the Holy Spirit is the exact same as God. And Jesus is the exact same as God. Therefore, Jesus is the exact same as the Holy Spirit. All three entities of the Trinity are the exact same as the other.

This is important as we continue to study the relationship of the three Godhead. Though we can make distinctions between

Them and see different things each One does for us, when it comes down to it, They are the exact same, because They are One. You are never wrong to only address One of Them, as it won't cause the other Two to be mad or refuse to help you, because They are One. If one particular Godhead terrifies you, rest assured that He is One and the things you love about one aspect hold true throughout Them all.

There is beauty in the different aspects of each member of the Trinity. Understanding more clearly the roles of the Father, Son, and Holy Spirit can help us more clearly to understand God.

God designed the earth to reflect heaven. God is a family-oriented God, and so the roles of our families today reflect the Godhead. This system where the earth reflects what is in heaven was made for a perfect world without sin, but sin entered and things got messed up. The earthly roles do not reflect the heavenly aspects as they were designed to do, and the effect is that individuals are left feeling hurt and abandoned by God. The heavenly is perfect; it does not change based on what the earthly does. The earthly is sinful, and so we sometimes get the wrong understanding of God because of the example we see on earth.

In the heaven, God has three parts—Father, Son, and Spirit. On earth, the Father is represented in our dads, the Son is represented in our friends and siblings, and the Spirit is represented in our moms.

Furthermore, we have three sets of needs—body, soul, and spirit. Our body needs are identity, provision, and protection and are taken care of by the Father. Our soul needs are communication and companionship, and they are taken care of by the Son. Our spirit needs are teaching, nurture, and comfort; and they are taken care of by the Spirit.[3]

Heavenly	Needs	Earthly
Father God	Body: identity, provision, and protection	Dads
Jesus	Soul: communication and companionship	Friends and siblings
Holy Spirit	Spirit: teaching, nurture, and comfort	Moms

Author's interpretation of the Father Ladder[4]

This system is not broken, but it is flawed because of human sin. The ways we see God are often a reflection of the earthly side of things. The examples we see in the earthly often bring damage to the way we see God, but it can also shed light on His character when people are living as sons and daughters.

Though the earthly system was designed after the heavenly, there need to be distinctions made between the two because earth is not a pure depiction of heaven due to sin. If we use the examples we see on earth to be the only way we know the heavenly, then our view of God is extremely broken.

The Father, Son, and Spirit do not change. They are not affected by the earthly and will always stay true to Their character.

> The Lord descended in the cloud and stood with him there, and proclaimed the name of the Lord. The Lord passed before him and proclaimed, "The Lord, the Lord, a God merciful and gracious, slow to anger, and abounding in steadfast love and faithfulness, keeping steadfast love for thousands, forgiving iniquity and transgression and sin, but who will by no means clear the guilty, visiting the iniquity of the fathers on the children and the children's children, to

the third and the fourth generation." (Exodus 34:5–7)

This is how the Lord identifies Himself. He is merciful. He is gracious. He is slow to anger. He is full of love. He is faithful. He loves the nations. He forgives sin. He is just.

Our God is good. He is kind and compassionate. He is omniscient, omnipresent, and omnipotent. He is divine. He is the Creator, the Healer, the Helper, the Savior, and the One True God.

The way you view God needs to be removed from the biases that you learned from the earthly. God is not your parents. God is not your siblings. God is not your friends. God is not solely represented by any one person or situation. Go back to the Source. Search for God in God, not in people. Learn who He is by what He is saying and doing, not by what people are saying and doing. Dig into the real character of God, and you will be pleasantly surprised.

When we learn God's character and begin to recognize all the things He has done for us, we can step into our identity and walk in the fullness of healing. When we know Him, we begin to know ourselves as He made us to be. When we see just how good our God truly is, a lot of questions and hurts and frustrations about this world and ourselves fall away, and we can rest in the truth of who He is.

Oh Papa, thank You for who You are. There aren't enough marvelous words to describe how good You are. Thank You. Thank You for Your character. Thank You for never changing; thank You for letting us start to glimpse Your glory. Father, heal our image of You. May we know who You really are and not be influenced by this world. May this world begin to reflect You more. Father, shock our hearts with new revelation of You. We put our faith in You and all that You say You are. You are good and worthy to be praised. We love You Father, and thank You for loving us.

Chapter 11

SHAMELESS

There is this common church phrase that I have recently come to hate. I used to use it all the time and thought that it was a great thing, especially for young girls. But then I realized some of the dangers of using it.

The phrase is "guard your heart." In principle, this is a good thing, but I think a lot of people go about it the wrong way. I know I did.

I took this phrase to mean that I needed to shut off all my emotions to certain things, especially people. I used this phrase to justify pushing people away and becoming a guarded and defensive person. I used it to say that having even a little bit of feeling or emotion was bad.

I also took this phrase to mean that I was the one who needed to do the guarding. I took my heart into my own hands and didn't let God have much of a say about it. I took control of my heart and declared that I was guarding it. But this taught me that God wasn't capable of guarding me. This taught me that I was alone in guarding something I don't even fully understand.

We guard our hearts through God's peace and truth. God crafted our hearts and is therefore the only one qualified to do any measure of protection over us. Emotions and feelings are not bad, and shutting them off is never the answer. But we don't let our emotions and feelings lead us. We need to place our hearts into the hands of the only Being that can take care of us fully.

After all, it's about Him, not us. Often, we get caught up in trying to fix something about ourselves, or trying to be better at something, or trying to do more. But we're missing the point. We try to search our own hearts and dig up what's bad in ourselves, but by doing this, we keep our focus upon ourselves.

> Search me, God, and know my heart; test
> me and know my anxious thoughts. See if there is
> any offensive way in me, and lead me in the way
> everlasting. (Psalm139:23–24 (NIV))

This needs to become our heart cry. Let God search you and know you. Let Him be the one to keep you in check and correct you. Fix your thoughts on Jesus, not your own improvement. Jesus is the Healer, Savior, and Advocate. Look to Him; focus on Him. It is not your job to search your heart—It's His. It is your job to search Him and His heart.

There's no need to fear His correction or guidance. He is gentle and kind. I have seen Him give correction to many people and have experienced it myself. He is so full of love that obedience is easy. His faithfulness and steadfastness make it easy to shed off anything that He declares is not of you.

One of the stories that demonstrate His correction so beautifully is the story of Hosea and Gomer. I recommend you read the Book of Hosea to get the whole story.

Hosea is a righteous man of God and a prophet. One day, God speaks to Hosea and tells him to go and marry a prostitute. Hosea obeys and finds Gomer. He marries her and brings her into his household. Remember how significant this is for Gomer—She was a woman without hope of a future and then a righteous man chooses to marry her. They have two sons and a daughter together, and Gomer is guaranteed an identity for the rest of her life.

Then one day, Gomer makes a mistake. She repeats the sins of her past and sleeps with a different man. Because of this sin, she is thrown out of her house and is being sold into slavery.

Hosea must have been devastated. The woman he made his wife, the one he loves and the mother of his children, betrayed him. He resigns to let his wife go into slavery because by law and tradition it is the right response.

Then, God speaks to Hosea and tells him to go buy his wife back. And Hosea obeys. Imagine the humiliation and reputation he was sacrificing to go and buy his own wife from an auction.

This is how God loves and corrects us. He buys us back every single time—without a second thought. And more than that, His love brings us to never repeat those sins. Gomer never runs away from home again. Our God's correction is full of tender love and compassion that leads us to know Him and allows us to learn our identity.

Correction from the Father is not a thing to fear. When He searches our hearts and guides us to Himself, He is showing us that we are valuable to Him. He wants nothing in the way of our relationship with Him, and He proves that to us time and time again.

Shame tries telling us this isn't the case. Shame would tell us that when we mess up, when we repeat the sins of our past, we're done. We're taken out of the game. We should hide and fear. Shame tells us to react and run.

Jesus's presence removes our shame.

> They went each to his own house, but Jesus went to the Mount of Olives. Early in the morning he came again to the temple. All the people came to him, and he sat down and taught them. The scribes and the Pharisees brought a woman who had been caught in adultery, and placed her in the midst they said to him, "Teacher, this woman has been caught in the act of adultery. Now in the Law Moses commanded us to stone such woman. So what do you say?" This they said

to test him, that they might have some charge to bring against him. Jesus bent down and wrote with his finger on the ground. And as they continued to ask him, he stood up and said to them, "Let him who is without sin among you be the first to throw a stone at her." And once more he bent down and wrote on the ground. But when they heard it, they went away one by one, beginning with the older ones, and Jesus was left alone with the woman standing before him. Jesus stood up and said to her, "Woman, where are they? Has no one condemned you?" She said, "No one, Lord." And Jesus said, "Neither do I condemn you; go, and from now on sin no more." (John 7:53–8:11)

This woman was caught in the middle of sex with a man she is not married to and drag into the middle of a large crowd. She is naked, she is a lawbreaker, and she is surrounded by religious people. Her eyes probably never leave the ground as she feels the weight of shame.

She feels the stares of the crowd upon her. She is naked and surrounded by men, some of which she has probably been with. The crowd may be screaming for righteousness, but they had wandering eyes and imaginations.

Jesus sees His daughter before Him. He sees the crowd looking at her. He knows the shame she carries. And He stays silent, but He moves.

People wonder what Jesus was writing, but I think the question is why. Why would He bend down and draw in the dirt? When Jesus started writing, He drew the eyes of the crowd onto Himself. The crowd stopped gawking at the naked woman and started to crane their necks to see what the Teacher was writing. He finally stands to answer the incessant questions, but then immediately bends down again to write more. He didn't give the crowd even a second to take their attention off of Him. He was fiercely protecting His daughter by using Himself as a distraction for the onlookers.

And when the crowd is gone, Jesus looks to His daughter. He asks her to say out loud the words that define His ministry.

Don't you see? There is no one who condemns you. Jesus has removed even the idea of shame, so stop living in it!

And God has always taken action to remove shame. Back in the garden, Adam and Eve make coverings for themselves out of fig leaves after they sin and realize their nakedness. These coverings had to have been nothing more than bikinis, covering only the bare minimum of their shame. But they don't even leave the garden of Eden in their shameful state.

> And the Lord God made for Adam and for his wife garments of skins and clothed them. (Genesis 3:21)

Some suggest that the skin used was from a lamb.[1] God removes the original shameful coverings and instead sends His children out under the blood of the Lamb. Even from the beginning, God covers our shame.

There is no one to condemn you because you are covered in the blood of the Lamb. There is no shame where there is no condemnation. God isn't interested in shaming us. He wants to love us and bless us. Seconds after the fall of man, He clothes Adam and Eve so that they can be unashamed.

Jesus's presence removes shame. And when a person feels no shame or condemnation, others around them notice.

In John 4, Jesus talks to the woman at the well. This woman is a prostitute and a shameful woman. We know because she has had multiple husbands and isn't even married to the man she is currently living with. We also know that she feels shame because she is drawing water in the middle of the day. The women would normally go to the well in the cool times, but this woman goes in the heat so as to avoid the women of her community.[2]

In the conversation they have, Jesus reveals how deeply He knows this woman. He longs for her to know Him and can't help but offer her the Living Water. She is deeply moved by all that Jesus tells her and even begins to wonder if He is the Messiah.

> So the woman left her water jar and went away into town and said to the people, "Come, see a man who told me all that I ever did. Can this be the Christ?" They went out of the town and were coming to him. (John 4:28–30)

Her response to Jesus is beautiful, and she wants others to know Him as well. What is incredible about this passage is that the people of the town listen to her. The people of the town knew this woman; they knew she was shameful and not respectable. And yet what was different about this woman after meeting Jesus that the town came to meet the person she now knows.

The woman at the well met Grace, and a whole town noticed. People notice when we are covered in the blood of the Lamb. Walk out of shame, as it is not for you. Every chance He got, Jesus worked to dispel shame, so stop trying to put it upon yourself.

We are not clothed in fig leaves; we are wrapped in the blood of the Lamb. Our sins are covered; there is no condemnation. Walk away from shame and never look back.

> *Jesus, thank You for Your kindness. Thank You for covering our shame and removing all condemnation. We boldly declare that we are not condemned! May we boldly approach Your thrown wrapped fully in Your blood. Jesus, rip away our shame and help us to never again accept it for ourselves. Father, we place everything we are into Your hands; You guard our hearts; You search our minds. We let go of control over ourselves, and we fix our thoughts on You. We can shamelessly sit with You as You guide us and perfect us in Your love. Thank You Jesus. We love You.*

Chapter 12

BUT JESUS

Sometimes, life just sucks. A lot of the time, people will shrug or sigh after they finish talking about their problems. Or they will finish their list of issues with the phrase "but, it's okay." This keeps our minds only on ourselves.

We need to finish sentences with a declaration of "but, Jesus . . ."

Psalm 22 is a foreshadow of the cross. It is the cry of our Savior Jesus as He suffers with us. And yet, in the midst of the anguish, Jesus praises the Lord in Heaven.

> My God, my God, why have you forsaken me? Why are you so far from saving me, from the words of my groaning? O my God, I cry by day, but you do not answer, and by night, but I find no rest.
>
> Yet you are holy, enthroned on the praises of Israel. (Psalm 22:1–3)

Verse 3 could also be written, "Dwelling in the praises of Israel." Our God is full of power, might, and authority; and yet He chooses to enthrone Himself on our praise. A king dwells where His throne is. Because our Lord chose to be enthroned upon our praise; as soon as we praise His name, He is there.

We need to constantly be praising our God. He is worthy of all praise; we can never give Him enough! By praising, we usher in more of His reign on earth and make way for the Kingdom to invade. The Kingdom increases when we give thanks and praise His name.

In all situations, lift up praise to the Father. No matter what circumstances you find yourself in, He is still good. Talking about our problems leaves us feeling empty and broken, but when we talk about Jesus and praise Him, we have no need to feel anything but joy and love. Learn how to keep the storm raging around you from becoming the storm inside you. Learn what stepping into peace looks like. Deeply discover the meaning of shalom.[1]

The gospel is Christ-centered. You are not the central part of the message that Jesus brought. Too often, we talk only about ourselves and don't ask God to bring His perspective and heart into the situation. When we wholeheartedly praise Him, we look past our earthly existence and are able to join eternity in praise for our good Father.

There are endless things to praise our God for. If you are having trouble thinking where to start, remember the cross. Remember who He says you are.

If you claim that you are simply a sinner saved by grace, you do not know who you are. This phrase is nowhere in the Bible. We are no longer sinners—We are saints. You are fully forgiven and you are no longer a sinner. You are a brand-new creation; saying you are a sinner but you are saved by grace is mixing your old self with your new self.[2]

Grace says that you are a saint. The phrase sinner saved by grace came around because we still sin in our daily lives, and so the question was raised if we are anything more than sinners. This cop-out phrase is an example of how we have taken the perfect theology of Jesus found in the Word and lowered it down to meet where we are. We need to believe what the Bible tells us and raise our experience up to meet it.

You are a saint. You are no longer a sinner. You may be thinking, "That can't be because I still sin."

> No one born of God makes a practice of sinning, for God's seed abides in him, and he cannot keep on sinning because he has been born of God. (1 John 3:9)

This is not saying that if you sin, you are not born of God. This verse means that when we sin, we step out of our identity. You are born of God and that will not change. When we sin, we operate outside of our true identity. I believe that if we had a complete revelation of who our God is and who He says we are, we would never sin again. But we do sin again, and we are instantly and completely forgiven. Because of Jesus, you are no longer a sinner, you are a saint.

Another "but, Jesus. . ." that should be more readily declared in our lives are the abundant blessings that we have already been given. We are blessed before we are sent. We are blessed before we do anything. We are blessed.

Blessings are not something we have to earn. We don't work for love, peace, forgiveness, or any other thing that Christ has already declared that we have. Believe what the Bible says, believe what Jesus said, for we have the full abundance of blessings that our God has. We already have them; we do not need to do anything to have them.

We don't work for love—We work from love.[3] We don't work for peace—We work from peace. We don't work for forgiveness—We work from forgiveness. A lot of times, we are trying to work for things we have already been given outright. Stop striving and just sit in the abounding blessings of our Lord.

Jesus is the reason for so many things that we get to receive. Jesus is the reason we can boldly and shamelessly approach the King. Jesus is the reason for any peace, rest, blessing, joy, and any good thing that we have.

Have a Christ-focused life, not a self-centered existence. Stop ending your sentences with excuses and start declaring His goodness into every area of your life.

Sometimes life sucks, but Jesus is good and has made the way clear for us to bring His Kingdom onto this earth, and He joyfully walks with us as we journey to deeper realms of knowing His love.

I need you to know that these aren't just pretty words on a page. I have walked through many things that should not bring joy, but have. I have seen people smile and laugh when there is no earthly reason why they should do so. I have seen pain and suffering engulf someone's life, one of these times being when my older sister received a heartbreaking diagnosis.

In May 2010, we received the initial diagnosis, and we were told my older sister would be dead in a couple months. A few weeks later they found the correct diagnosis, and we learned that she had a large cell tumor in her tailbone.

June 2010, she had surgery to remove it, and they believed they got it all.

August 2010, she began treatment at MD Anderson because it was back. Treatment included monthly injections, and after quite a bit of time the tumor was calcified and went into remission.

January 2012, it was back. Treatment became daily self-injections, for an 18-year-old girl afraid of needles.

July 2015, she was finally able to stop all treatment because there had been no change in the tumor for a year.

March 2016, it came back and treatment included a year worth of surgeries.

Through this entire time there were multiple drugs and treatments used for pain management, and yet she was still in constant pain. Her nerves and spine have taken large amounts of damage and it is unsure if her body will ever function completely normal again.

Currently, April 2017, she is still fighting pain and nerve damage, but she does it newly married and with a smile, in true Stefanie fashion.

Everyone in my family has been affected by this sickness, but we have all found new strength through it. I have included excerpts from my Mom's journal during the time of treatment, as well as an essay written by my younger Sister. My family isn't perfect, but I hope you see that it is possible to praise our Lord even in the brokenness of this earth.

Journal entry by Kim Renkema – 11/9/2010

Just so you are warned: This is a very un-Kim like update...

So I was asked this week if I've at least been able to see God thru all of this. My immediate in my head response was, nope, not yet, still waiting. My head edited that response because of course I work at a church and that couldn't possibly be my response. So I said, "sometimes, but not always, I'm sure at the end of it His plans will be abundantly clear". She told me that that would be her prayer, that we see God. In my head, I was thinking, great, but what about the pain, don't forget to pray that the pain goes away!

I've been wrestling with this question for a few days now. And yes, God is all over it but...

A lot of days my prayers start with – OK God – here's what I need today. Or the days where I'm figuratively stomping my feet and saying I know you can do it, so JUST TAKE AWAY THE PAIN!!! NOW!!! It's like I'm 2 all over again. Or the days I avoid the tasks I need to do because I just don't wanna. Or thinking, really, now my best friend has cervical cancer, you must be kidding. Or please just sell our old house; we are drowning with medical bills, travel expenses and 2 houses. Or lastly, ok, what more do You have today for me.

I bought a sign last week and hung it over the new kitchen sink "FAITH – makes things possible, not easy". Talk about true!! Nothing about this is easy. Watching your kid writhe on the ground in pain and there is NOTHING you can do. Watching all of her friends do normal 16-year-old things while they slowly forget to keep in touch with her because she just isn't up to do much. It's like it would be easier if she was sicker because people would keep in touch or check on her, but since we know she will be ok, for now she's kind of been on her own. I'm sure the days she goes to school are not great either; the high school is a big place and there are a lot of kids she doesn't know in her classes. In the past she would have made friends of them all. Now she feels bad and is just getting by and she's on her own. Please don't miss understand, I'm so thankful that perhaps this will all be behind us in a couple years, but the oncologist always reminds us it is a lesson in patience and could be 2 years or more until things start to work, or the tumor is in remission, or dare I say, life might return to normal?

This experience has introduced us to a whole new world. I now check regularly on 3 pages of kids with caring bridge sites. Before May of this year, I only knew one sweet boy at church that had a site; now I pray regularly for many of them that have very serious life threatening illnesses. I had no idea that The National Cancer Institute's (NCI) budget is currently $4.6 billion. Of that, breast cancer receives 12%, prostate cancer receives 7% and all 12 major groups of pediatric cancers COMBINED received less than 3%. It's the #1 disease killer of kids yet receives less than 3% of cancer funding and SO FEW even know about this!! I actually almost get angry at all the pink ribbons for breast cancer – what about the kids?!? I'm not sure what to do about this information, I'm not normally the one to be the outspoken advocate; is that part of the end result in this? The only thing that makes Stefanie's tumor not cancer is the fact that is benign. My heart breaks for many of these families; I'm sure we are only feeling a portion of what they go through.

Up until this year we have been EXTREMLY blessed with nothing major in our lives; we're boring and average. My husband introduced me to Christ in 1990. Before that I had never been to church and been told very little about Jesus. I learned growing up that I'll just take care of myself. Learning to fully give it all to Christ is a lesson I still at times have to work on. I've looked at other families and thought – wow! They are so strong. I wonder what I'd be like in that situation. That doesn't mean I really wanted to find out! So here we are. Greg and I have had many conversations about – what did we do, we can't handle this, did God get the right family? Recently our Children's Ministry staff was studying Beth Moore; the topic of the day was Lessons Paul learned from hardships in Asia. Here were the profound things God words said to me that day.

Sometimes we are being the most powerfully used when we face the most difficulty.

The enemy can't squelch the Power of God so he tries to disable the servant.

Even the most devoted believers can encounter hardships FAR BEYOND our ability to endure.

The original Greek word for despair means "to be wholly without resource"; been there AND got the t-shirt.

2 Corinthians 1:8-11 We do not want you to be uninformed, brothers and sisters, about the troubles we experienced in the province of Asia. We were under great pressure, far beyond our ability to endure, so that we despaired of life itself. Indeed, we felt we had received the sentence of death. But this happened that we might not rely on ourselves but on God, who raises the dead. He has delivered us from such a deadly peril, and he will deliver us again. On him we have set our hope that he will continue to deliver us, as you help us by your prayers. Then many will give thanks on our behalf for the gracious favor granted us in answer to the prayers of many.

Here is what I heard, God won't give us temptation beyond what we can handle (1 Corinthians 10:13 No temptation has overtaken you except what is common to mankind. And God is faithful; he will not let you be tempted beyond what you can bear. But when you are tempted, he will also provide a way out so that you can endure it), however, he may allow us to have great trials and it is our responsibility to Glorify Him in it.

So back to the very original question that started this, I've been compiling my list in my head of all the places that we've seen God during all of this:

Our new house is beautiful and peaceful and we are blessed (We thought we had all we could handle with the move and building Greg's dad an apartment onto the new house and the actual move, hmm..)

My staff has been amazing and covered for me for all the time I've missed work or my head hasn't been in the game or I've just been cranky

The original surgery that went well to remove the tumor

The basket of goodies that included an amazing blanket to cover my daughter in The Word that my friends carried to my car as we rushed off to our appointments in OKC

A text message that read, "It's ok, even when you don't have the words, relax, the rest of us will cover her in prayer"

All the doctors that moved quickly from diagnoses, to treatment, to get us to MD Anderson, to all the other additional doctors and medical staff

All the people that have helped us resolve insurance and drug issues

The drug company actually delivering the last medicine without daily phone calls

Dr. Hughes & Dr. Mason who have both been AMAZING to Stefanie

Our sweat church friend who is also a nurse and offered to give Stefanie her injections so she and I wouldn't have to

Asbury youth staff being as concerned for Stefanie as we are

Greg & I having strength during different times of this journey to lend the other support

Melissa and Nicole having compassion for their sister and being able to continue with normal daily teenage life

God's Word: Jeremiah 29:11 For I know the plans I have for you," declares the LORD, "plans to prosper you and not to harm you, plans to give you hope and a future."

And I'm sure there are so many more that I either forgot to record or perhaps didn't even recognize. I'm sure there will still be days that I'm frustrated and forget to see God in the little things, but I've never wavered on if He is there or not, if He has a plan or not; I'm sure this journey would be so much harder without him walking with us. It doesn't mean I want get anxious or wish that our timing was also His. I know, even if I don't understand it, He loves Stefanie even more than I do. It also doesn't mean that there will be days that I don't miss my easy going, happy go lucky Stefanie; but I can't wait to see what He has in store for her life; it must be something AMAZING.

Isaiah 40:31 But those who hope in the LORD will renew their strength. They will soar on wings like eagles; they will run and not grow weary, they will walk and not be faint.

Journal entry by Kim Renkema – 5/19/2015

Today our youngest daughter, Nicole, graduates from High School. It has been quite enjoyable to get a school year with just Nicole at home. Greg and I are excited to move into the empty nest stage of life. It makes the times they all come home to visit so much more important.

Today also marks the five-year anniversary of Stefanie's diagnoses of her giant cell tumor. How is it that one-day's activities are so exactly marked in our memory? We had very recently purchased our house and that day we were signing the contract for the addition so that Greg's dad could live with us. Technically, on this day, we received a misdiagnosis for her previous four weeks of pain, but it was the start of this five-year journey for us. We would rush to OKC twice for biopsies looking for correct answers. June 1, 2010 was her removal surgery and on June 5, 2010, she turned 16. It wasn't until August that we knew the tumor was not gone and she would begin seeking treatment at MD Anderson.

I cannot say that these five years have been easy. This kind of disease takes its toll on every family member. There are struggles that never get talked about. There are hurts and issues that it is just easier to stuff than deal with. Moreover, you would certainly never air the pain and the dirty laundry to the public, sometimes not even to friends. However, most of the time, we remember to lay it all at the cross in order to continue to put one foot in front of the other. I have the advantage of occasionally being able to forget that Stefanie still has constant pain and many struggles. She does not have that. However, her continued desire to seek God in all things constantly amazes me!

Matthew 11:28-30 Then Jesus said, "Come to me, all of you who are weary and carry heavy burdens, and I will give you rest. Take my yoke upon you. Let me teach you, because I am humble and gentle at heart, and you will find rest for your souls. For my yoke is easy to bear, and the burden I give you is light."

Matthew 6:33 Seek the Kingdom of God above all else, and live righteously, and he will give you everything you need.

So, where are we today? We don't update as often because you just learn that all of this is your new normal. We still fight with drug companies, Stef still gets epidurals regularly for the pain, and many other things that aren't so new anymore so we don't report on them, but they still happen. And that's okay.

Cancer by Nicole Renkema, December 2013

How would you describe cancer? Is it just a disease in a person's body that only affects the person with the illness? Cancer can tear a family apart, and it has a traumatic effect on not only the afflicted person, but also the family and friends. Even when people win the battle of cancer, they still lose so much. Society has become almost numb to the idea of cancer until they are directly affected by it.

The dictionary defines cancer as a serious disease caused by cells that are not normal and can spread to one or many parts of the body. However, I define it as breath taking, beautiful, and strong.

BUT JESUS

My Grandmother Renkema was one of the strongest woman I knew. She is one of the reasons why I would define cancer as strength. My Grandmother was diagnosed with breast cancer and there was not one day that she did not put her best foot forward and try to make the best of it. One of the quotes my Grandmother showed me when I was young was: "He gives strength to the weary and increases the power of the weak. Isaiah 40:29". Even through the chemo, which is the treatment of disease by means of chemicals that have a specific toxic effect upon the disease-producing microorganisms or that selectively destroy cancerous tissue, she kept going. And then two years later when she got lung cancer too, she never gave up. Cancer is the smile on my grandmother's face even when the chemotherapy was killing her inside.

The affects cancer has on families and friends can be breath taking. Cancer is the moment when my mom calls me during school to tell me that my Aunt had been diagnose with cancer; she was really my Mom's best friend Heidi, but I think of her as my Aunt. That's breathtaking. The moment that absolutely took my breath away is on the day of my Aunt's final chemotherapy, the day she was able to say that she is a cancer survivor. As she walked through the doors of the Tulsa Cancer Center in Oklahoma, I know she just sighed the biggest sigh of relief, that she will be able to wake up and not have to put on a wig, or just wake up in misery. Cancer is also the breathtaking moment when my Aunt took me out for lunch and told me that the cancer had returned in her body and it was spreading rapidly. She died not long after that.

Finally, I define cancer as beautiful. At sixteen years old the doctor found a tumor on my sister Stefanie's tailbone. My sister is always so bubbly and full of life; she always tries to put a smile on her face. Even though she is losing her hair from the chemotherapy like treatment she is in, she still manages to put on the best outfits and makes herself look absolutely beautiful. How even when she is deathly afraid of needles and she is giving herself an injection to shrink the tumor, she still manages to give me a wink to let me know that she is okay.

There are many forms of cancer, but in the end, it effects more people than people think. My Grandma, Aunt, and Sister would not be the same women as they are today if they did not have to face cancer. My Aunt was one of the strongest women I knew, and now I realize it was selfish of me to be so distraught over my Aunt's death. Because now she is out of pain, out of misery, and now she is looking down upon me and being my Guardian Angel for me. Lives have been lost and tears have been shed, but in the end, I am so glad these women have been in my life and I have been able to build a relationship with them while I could. You could look at cancer in a positive or a negative way, but I like to look at it as breath taking, beautiful, and strong.

Jesus, thank You. Thank You for Your faithfulness and Your goodness. Teach us to always look to you no matter the circumstances. Teach us to praise Your name no matter what. Thank You for choosing to be enthroned on our praises. Lord, dwell among us as we daily increase our praise to You. Shape our hearts after Yours and always remind us of the things You have already done for us. Help us believe everything the Bible says and everything You continue to say over us. May we stop trying to work for things that we have already been given. Let us be a people operating out of Your love, because You already love us, just as we are.

Iron

Chapter 13

RESET

Therefore, brothers, since we have confidence to enter the holy places by the blood of Jesus, by the new and living way that he opened for us through the curtain, that is, through his flesh, and since we have a great priest over the house of God, let us draw near with a true heart in full assurance of faith, with our hearts sprinkled clean from an evil conscience and our bodies washed with pure water. Let us hold fast the confession of our hope without wavering, for he who promised is faithful. And let us consider how to stir up one another to love and good works, not neglecting to meet together, as is the habit of some, but encouraging one another, and all the more as you see the Day drawing near. (Hebrews 10:19–25)

We are designed for relationship. Our God is highly relational and created us to be in union and connection with Him and others. You have a type of relationship with everyone around you, but you choose who you form community with. Relationships lend to community when people find others that have things in common with themselves

Community is an incredible gift from the Father, but things can stand in the way of genuine community. Before we move forward, there is something that you must get rid of.

Pride is the number one killer of community. It is nearly impossible for other people to be able to disarm our pride. You must be the one to lay down your pride, turn 180 degrees, and never look back.

Pride is a liar and will hinder you from having meaningful relationships. Pride keeps you from asking for help when you are desperate. Pride keeps you from needed correction and guidance. Pride keeps you isolated. Pride keeps you from seeing the work that God is doing. Pride shuts the Kingdom door.

Pride is a liar, for it tells us we are the only ones capable of doing a task. No person can stand on their own feet. The Bible so clearly emphasizes the importance of community. Jesus sends out the disciples two by two, just as the animals entered Noah's ark two by two. Eve was created soon after Adam because it is not good for us to be alone.

You need genuine and sincere friends to help you in life. You cannot do this on your own—No one can. And even bigger than the scope of your life, the Great Commission and the mandate that God has placed on the Church cannot be completed by just one person.

We are built for community. In our very DNA, we are wired to connect with people. Community is one of the most important blessings and weapons that our Lord has given us. And because community is so vital, it is often ruthlessly targeted by the enemy.

Our connection with the people around us is bombarded with satan's lies. Comparison is one major way community is damaged. Comparison comes from the lie that says you are not special. We all long to be unique and individual. We love to say how much God loves the people around us, but we often turn around and wish that we too could be loved by God the way that other people are.

Dear friend, run as fast as you can from this lie that says you are not special. Stop saying that God loves equally, because He does not.

Saying that God's love is equal for all people puts a measurement on Him. Our God is immeasurable. There is no way to quantify Him.[1]

God loves uniquely.[2] He loves you in a way so individual to your heart that only you can fully know Him in this way. Stop trying to get what others have and run after the treasures that He has designed specifically for you.

Learning how to see the ways the Father loves you uniquely is vital to maintaining meaningful friendships. I have a dear friend that I have known for a long time. We have walked through many challenges together and have a lot in common. And sometimes we feel like we have too much in common. We are both academic, we both love reading and writing, we both love pouring into students, we both work in the same ministries, we both paint, we both love music, and I could go on with the things that we have in common. Our friendship is strong because we do so much of the same things, but the enemy loves to use this against us.

We both go through times when we get into comparing ourselves to the other. There have been so many occasions that I am consumed with the idea that my friend is better than me in all the things that we have in common, and this makes me want to retreat from her companionship as well as stop doing those things that I love. This lie has wiggled into our friendship and done damage to both of us. In order to combat this, we have had to have open and vulnerable conversations about these fears and hurts. We have to recognize that because together we are advancing the Kingdom, the enemy tries to get us working against each other.

In my own heart, I get the most jealous when I start looking at the ways Jesus so sweetly loves my friend. I look at how incredible she is and tell myself I will never measure up to her. I look at how preciously Jesus pursues her heart and feel inadequate because He doesn't talk to me about those exact same things. But when I do this I rob my own relationship with the Father. By looking at what my friend gets, I can't see the ways that I am being loved and pursued.

The Father loves His children in ways so unique to each individual heart that only you can see the ways that He loves you fully. The blessings and treasures He designs for you can only be accepted by you. By seeking the ways that you are uniquely loved, you can begin to flourish as you experience how the Father so loves you. Learn how to cherish and hold dear the little ways that your God daily reminds you how special you are to Him. By loving us uniquely, our good Father shows us just how intimately He knows our hearts and reminds us that we don't have to fight other people to get His love and attention.

People are not a threat to your salvation. People are not a threat to the things God has for you. People are not a threat to you. Your worth and identity are not affected by any other person, nor do your worth and identity affect other people. Our worth is solely wrapped up in Jesus Christ, and our identity is determined only by our Heavenly Father. Other people having something is not going to affect your ability to get it. And so often the things the Father does have for you are so much better than what other people appear to have. The storehouses of heaven are endless, and you have access to them.

The Bible is clear on how we are to treat people. We are to love our enemy.[3] We are to be good neighbors.[4] We are to wholeheartedly love one another.[5] Nowhere does it say that people are a threat to us. In fact, we are told that our fight is not against flesh and blood.[6]

We need to have respect and honor for the people in our lives. Honor those around you by listening to what they have to say with an open mind. Respect them by not trying to argue them out of their opinions. You don't have to agree with everything someone says, but you do have to love them no matter what they say. Be willing to just listen instead of offering advice or correcting. Be less ready to share your own opinion, and just share Jesus. Read Romans 14 and remember it when you want everyone to think the exact same way that you do.

Respect what insights other people can give you. We all have the same Spirit. Every Christian is carrying around the same manifestation of God. Even little ones are given the same Spirit that adults have. Don't stifle the wisdom of God because you think someone is too young to have good wisdom. Don't shut down the Kingdom by letting your dislike of someone keep you from appreciating what revelations they may have to share. Don't let your pride tell you that you are the only person who can hear good news from God. A lot of the times, other people's opinions can help you shape and understand your own beliefs better and help you do more digging and research into the Father.

At the end of the day, the only people who need to be okay with your decisions are you and God. This does not give you a license to hurt people, but it does mean that you don't have to work your whole life for the approval of man. You live for an audience of One. The things you do in your life will affect the people around you, but the only Person that you must give account to at the end of it all is Jesus. Keep your eyes on the King, for whatever you do unto man, you do unto the Lord.[7]

> *Jesus, reset our mind-set on community. Set things right within us and fill us with truth so that our community with one another may reflect You. Teach us to love one another as You love us. Thank You for the ability to have deep connections with people. Thank You for the blessing of genuine community. I declare that anything standing in the way of us having deep community be removed so that we may glorify You in our relationships. Father, may we love, honor, and respect every single one of Your created children. As we learn to love, I break off any desire for people pleasing. Teach us to live for an audience of One so that we are free to love abundantly.*

Chapter 14

HEARTBEAT

We long to be people who lean so closely into Jesus that we can hear His heartbeat. And as we hear the rhythm of His heart, we feel the deep longing that Christ has for all people.

Our God is a missionary God. He longs for all people and all nations to know His name. He draws people into Himself and goes out to bring people to Him. Our God genuinely loves all people, and as His children, we need to be the same way.

The Old Testament is riddled with stories of God setting Himself apart from all other gods and making a great name for Himself. Jesus came and gave us a new covenant, and now, we are the ones who are to be going out and making His name famous.

The mandate we are given is so completely tied to other people that there is no denying that we are to be spreading His love to every person we encounter.

The Great Commandment:

> And one of the scribes came up and heard them disputing with one another, and seeing that he [Jesus] answered them well, asked him, "Which commandment is the most important of all?" Jesus answered, "The most important is, 'Hear, O Israel: The Lord our God, the Lord is

one. And you shall love the Lord your God with all your heart and with all your soul and with all your mind and with all your strength.' The second is this: 'You shall love your neighbor as yourself.' There is no other commandment greater than these." (Mark 12:28–31)

The Great Commission:

And Jesus came and said to them [the eleven disciples], "All authority in heaven and on earth has been given to me. Go therefore and make disciples of all nations, baptizing them in the name of the Father and of the Son and of the Holy Spirit, teaching them to observe all that I have commanded you. And behold, I am with you always, to the end of the age." (Matthew 28:18–20)

The Great Commandment and the Great Commission walk hand in hand.[1] We can't do one without the other, and both are necessary in order to continue the work Christ started. We are to make disciples. We are to equip the saints.

With Christ as our center, we work to bring people into the Kingdom. However, it is hard to do this when we are bad brothers.

The story of the Prodigal Son is found in Luke 15:11–32. The story is about two sons, in which one asks for his inheritance and leaves home. This brother spends all the money and eventually finds himself poor and feeding pigs until he decides to go to his father and ask for forgiveness. The other son stays with his father the entire time. This brother works for his father, never leaves home, and has no need of asking for forgiveness. When the prodigal son comes back to the family, there is a feast thrown in celebration because the father is elated that his son is back. The other brother, however, is upset and keeps himself outside of the party because he is mad that his wayward brother gets a party when he never did. The father comes to his son and asks him to celebrate the fact that his brother is home.

We have all been both brothers. Both of these gentlemen are good sons. The one who never leaves is a good son because he stays with his father. And the other is made a good son when he is redeemed by his father's embrace. But these gentlemen are bad brothers. The one who left never asks forgiveness from his brother, while the one who stayed refuses to celebrate the redemption of his brother.

So often we are good sons, but bad brothers. We love God, but we refuse to celebrate the people around us.

Jesus tells another parable in Matthew 20:1–16. This parable talks about a man who owns a vineyard and hires workers to reap the harvest. The owner pays all workers the same amount, no matter what time they began to work. All the workers are good sons because they labor for the Father. However, the workers who worked all day are upset that those who started later and only worked one hour get the same pay as themselves. They are being bad brothers.

Jesus came to teach us to be good brothers, as well as good sons. In Luke 4, Jesus has just started His ministry. In Luke 4:16–30 Jesus goes to Nazareth and teaches in his hometown for the first time. He stands before the people He grew up with, their full attention on Him, and He shows them His heart.

He first tells them how He fulfills the scriptures, and then in verse 24, He shocks them with what He says.

> And he said, "Truly, I say to you, no prophet is acceptable in his hometown. But in truth, I tell you, there were many widows in Israel in the days of Elijah, when the heavens were shut up for three years and six months, and a great famine came over all the land, and Elijah was sent to none of them but only to Zarephath, in the land of Sidon, to a woman who was a widow. And there were many lepers in Israel in the time of the prophet Elisha, and none of them was cleansed but only Naaman the Syrian." When they heard these things, all in the synagogue were filled with wrath. And they rose up and drove him out of

the town and brought him to the brow of the hill on which their town was built, so that they could throw him down the cliff. But passing through their midst, he went away. (Luke 4:24–30)

These women that Jesus talks about, Zarephath and Naaman, were Gentiles. Jesus is speaking to a room of Jews, and He tells them about Gentiles receiving healing and blessing instead of Jews. The Jews listening to Jesus get so mad that they try to kill Him. This crowd was full of good sons of God, but terrible brothers.

Salvation is for everyone. Jesus is for everyone—Jews, Gentiles, men, women, young, and old; people of any color, nationality, education, occupation, and opinion; people who have committed the worst crimes; and people who have committed no wrong. There is no exception to whom the Good News is for.

Quit being bad brothers to people who are not like you, or to people who have hurt you, or to people who you think are weird or different or bad or scary.

There is great joy in heaven when any person turns to God.

Just so, I tell you, there is joy before the angels of God over one sinner who repents. (Luke 15:10)

You are keeping yourself out of the celebration when you are mad at the blessing and salvation of others. You keep yourself out of the Kingdom when you act like a bad brother. Learn to celebrate any and every person. Learn to rejoice with those around you, despite any circumstance you find yourself in. It is important to be a good son, but it is just as important to be a good brother.

If you are about to justify yourself by asking who even is your brother, rest assured because Jesus has already answered this question. *The Parable of the Good Samaritan* is found in Luke 10:25–37, and it already tells us who our brothers are; they just call them neighbors.

We ask Jesus, "Who is my neighbor? Who is my brother?" Through the teaching of the good Samaritan, Jesus once again flips everything upside down. Jesus changes our mind-set and changes the question. It is no longer, "Who is my neighbor?" The question has become: "How can I be a neighbor?"[2]

Look for ways to help and encourage those around you. Love unabashedly and profoundly. Lower your expectations of what you can get from others, and raise your commitment to be a good brother to every person you encounter.[3]

The Kingdom is made of brothers living together as sons of God. Learn how to join this community and hear His resounding heartbeat for every person that walks this earth.

> *Jesus, we want to hear your heartbeat. We want to feel for people the way you do. Teach us to lean in so close to You that our love for our brothers is genuine and pure. Give us Your heart so that we can do the tasks You have started for us. Mold us into good sons and good brothers. Teach us to celebrate every breakthrough and blessing that the people around us receive, even if we are still waiting on our own. Teach us to join the celebration. I declare that we never again keep ourselves out of the party that we are invited to. Jesus, we ask for more of You. Thank You for giving us the right teachings and give us the strength and courage to become the people You long for us to be.*

Chapter 15

UNCOMMON

In Acts 10:9–16, Peter has a vision. In this vision, Peter is given permission to eat any and all food that he would desire. Peter objects, sticking to the Jewish laws, and says in verse 14, "By no means, Lord; for I have never eaten anything that is common or unclean." The response he is given is astounding. In verse 15, the voice answers him, saying: "What God has made clean, do not call common."

But this is not meant only to be applied to food. While Peter is digesting this vision, he is visited by men representing a reputable man named Cornelius who summons Peter to come to his house. The next day, Peter sets out with the men to the house of this God-fearing centurion.[1]

By the time Peter arrives, Cornelius has gathered his entire household to hear what Peter has to say.

> And he [Peter] said to them, "You your-selves know how unlawful it is for a Jew to asso-ciate with or to visit anyone of another nation, but God has shown me that I should not call any person common or unclean. So when I was sent for, I came without objection. I ask then why you sent for me." (Acts 10:28–29)

Peter continues and shares the Good News with the Gentiles before him. The people were ripe for the message, and the Holy Spirit falls onto the Gentiles.[2] This sets the Church up to bring the message of the cross to people of every nation. The Jewish laws were extremely strict, but truly a new covenant was established with the death and resurrection of Jesus. Everyone is given the chance to be completely clean the moment they profess that Jesus died in their place on the cross and profess Him as the Son of God.

What God has made clean do not call common. Every single person has been made clean. The cross was sufficient to make every sinner white and pure. Do not call anyone common.

We are all divinely created. Every life is stitched together by God. Jesus completely defeated death and now longs for everyone to be drawn to Him. No person, without exception, is common.

People don't yet know our God because we aren't showing Him to them. We treat people as commoners unless they profess Christ. And even then, we more readily offer criticism and punishment instead of encouragement.

We need to be calling out the greatness that is within every person. This is not done through relentless fault-finding. I am not saying to never give correction, but I am saying that degrading people will never give them room to step into their true identity.

Treat people like they have already been made perfect in Christ. See the greatness stored in everyone and pull it out by treating people as if they are already completely transformed into their original design—blameless, pure, and beautiful. Stop trying to dig up something you can offer people, and start asking God what He has to say to people.

Treat people as if they are already at the finish line hugging Jesus. Love people like they have never and could never hurt you. This is the sort of love that will bring people into believing that they can be the person they were created to be.

People act the way they do because they don't know any different. People mimic the things they have seen and will continue to live this way until something shows them that there is a different way.

Be different. Be the person that makes someone finally believe in themselves. Mimic Christ whom you know so that others may see Him too.

Because this world is looking for something different. In Luke 19:1–10, Zacchaeus climbs a sycamore tree to be able to see Jesus pass by. Zacchaeus is a tax collector and hated by many because of this. He is common and yet desires like so many to see this Man that people have been talking about. It should be noticed that the type of tree he climbs is a sycamore tree. The sycamore was the most common type of tree in that region at that time. So why even mention what type of tree Zacchaeus climbed into? Because people are looking for Jesus in common places.

You are surrounded by people who are looking for the Savior, whether they know it or not. And this world needs something different. Be uncommon because you are clean.

> *Jesus, thank You for making us clean. Forgive us for anyway we have treated clean things common. We repent Father, renew our minds so that we may see people as You see them. Show us Your heart for each individual person so that we can treat them as You treat them. Let us spark one another on to greatness and call out the light that is within every person. Jesus, may we be different so that the world may see You. Give us Your heart for people and the nations. Papa, we love You and we love Your people. Thank You for calling us children and help us treat every single person like they are a dear child of Yours, because they are.*

Chapter 16

APPLE TREES

What is the fruit of an apple tree? You're probably thinking, "Apples, duh." But are apples the ultimate fruit of the apple tree?

Buried inside the core of an apple, the part we throw away, are seeds. Those seeds are protected and carried by the physical fruit of the apple. And those seeds are created to be planted and cultivated to eventually produce another thriving apple tree.

When trees grow and produce apples, they are not thinking about how shiny, tasty, and nutritious their apples will be. They are thinking about how they can get their seeds spread and planted. Trees are worried about expanding the garden, and they do that through producing apples with good seeds inside.

And so, the fruit of an apple tree is more apple trees.

And we are to be a people who bear much fruit. When we live wrapped in the Father, we can't help but see good fruit in our lives. Through communing with the Holy Spirit, we produce the fruit of the Spirit, and that fruit can be seen and consumed by the people around us. Bearing good fruit is not bad, and in fact, it glorifies the Father.

> By this my Father is glorified, that you bear
> much fruit and so prove to be my disciples. (John
> 15:8)

Bearing fruit is good and pleasing, but individual fruit is not the ultimate goal. Bearing good fruit is simply a means to a greater end. Our individual fruit is to be used to bring more people into the Kingdom.

> And God blessed them. And God said to them, "Be fruitful and multiply." (Genesis 1:28A)

> And you, be fruitful and multiply, increase greatly on the earth and multiply in it. (Genesis 9:7)

The first part of the command is to bear fruit, but the second is to multiply. We are to be fruitful and, through it, multiply those who follow Jesus. We are to reproduce around us the good works and grace that have been worked within us. The commands we have are to love God above all and to help others love God. We do the second by letting the fruit of the first be evident in our lives. Our fruit draws and entices people to know Jesus. Our fruit awakens an appetite in others to experience something different. Through our fruit, we plant seeds that can lead to people growing into strong and healthy apple trees, which is what we are told to do.

> Go therefore and make disciples of all nations, baptizing them in the name of the Father and of the Son and of the Holy Spirit, teaching them to observe all that I have commanded you. And behold, I am with you always, to the end of the age. (Matthew 28:19–20)

> And he said to them, "Follow me, and I will make you fishers of men." (Matthew 4:19)

The Gospel we know and love should not stop at ourselves. The Gospel message is for us fully, and as we accept it and live it, it fully becomes our message for others. The Gospel came to you on its way to someone else. Continue planting seeds, cultivating the garden of the Kingdom of Heaven.

Individual fruit is good and needed, but there is a reason why when we walk in our identity, we produce fruit. Are you in the work of having good apples, or do you long to spread seeds and see trees as a result of your own fruit?

> *Jesus, thank You for the ability to bear fruit. Thank You for designing us to be able to draw people to You. Teach us how to look for fruit beyond ourselves; teach us how to produce more trees. We long to expand Your garden; show us how. May we take seriously our responsibility to teach people how to follow You. May we continue spreading the Gospel, knowing that it is for all people. Thank You for Your grace and kindness as we learn how to be people who spread Your love instead of letting it stop with us. Shape our hearts to be like Yours as we long for more people to know and love You as we do. Help us be fruitful and multiply.*

Kingdom Thinking

Chapter 17

SHEEPFOLD

I love that Jesus calls Himself the Good Shepherd. He is our Shepherd and we are His sheep. Of all the creatures we could have been likened to, I'm glad that we are sheep. Sheep may have a few weird quirks, but they are incredible examples of how we are to live in the Kingdom.

For example, sheep refuse to walk into darkness; they will only walk towards light. Sheep prefer to walk uphill rather than downhill, and they are more inclined to walk into the wind rather than with it.

We are to be people who refuse to partner with darkness—people who only walk in light. We move upward always because He takes us from glory to glory.[1] We walk against the forces of this world, but it is worth the effort as we live with our Lord.

Sheep are vulnerable creatures, especially during the first 24 hours of life. Sheep, and many other species, need to consume colostrum very quickly after birth. Colostrum is the first milk that a mother will have, and it is full of immunoglobulins that give passive immunity to the babies, which greatly increases their chance of survival and gives them a needed boost to start their life. Sheep are often born in the winter and can be born in freezing temperatures. If a lamb does not get proper warmth at birth, they can easily have their internal body temperature drop way below critical. When a shepherd finds a newborn lamb in such a critical condition, he has to work quickly. The shepherd knows that the lamb needs colostrum, but if he was to feed the colostrum with the low body temperature, it would shock the lamb's system and cause instant death. Therefore, a shepherd will take precious hours to raise the lamb's temperature before giving the life-altering colostrum.

We are fragile beings, and in many stages of our lives, we are like newborn lambs. Many times, we need first milk blessings that will change everything for us; but often, we may not be set up to receive these. The Lord God knows what you need, on every scale. He longs to bless you, but if you receive something you are not ready for, it will be useless. Trust God's timing. Rest in the fact that He plans on blessing you. He may be waiting so that you may see the fullness of His glory along with knowing His love deeper. Wait upon the Lord, for He is good.

Sheep have several blind spots, including directly behind them. Their range of vision behind and around them is affected by the length of their wool. For this reason, and to help them from over-heating, sheep's wool needs to be sheared. The shearing does not hurt; it is actually a relief for them to have the weight of the wool taken away. The wool constantly grows, and so shearing is done once or twice a year.

We are to be completely blind to our past sins. Our Lord forgets our sins, and we are invited to as well. We are to be a people who can no longer physically see the mistakes that lay behind us. But as we do reflect on our lives, we are able to see the Shepherd's continued faithfulness, goodness, and provision that can be seen clearly when looking at things from a distance and with new perspective. Shearing can also be seen as pruning. Trimming away the old is not a bad thing. Jesus offers to lighten us of things that don't fit with Him. It is a joy to be taken care of so intimately that He continuously works to keep us connected to Him. Let Him have His way deeper within you. Let Him remove things that you no longer need. Jesus isn't picking on you. He's making your life with Him more comfortable and shaping you into what He has designed you to be.

Sheep do not take care of themselves well. They won't sleep or eat unless they feel safe and will eat terrible things if they aren't guided to good forage. This is why the shepherd is so important. Sheep need constant care and would not survive without an attentive shepherd. They know where their safety comes from, and they grow to be completely dependent on the shepherd that takes care of them.

Rest knowing that you have a Good Shepherd who knows what you need. He guides us daily and is active in our lives. Jesus fully plans on preparing for you the things you need. He is our fortress and our strength. He is safe and we have no need for caution when we walk with Him.

Sheep trust the shepherd to lead them to good pasture, where they will then eat. The sheep feed themselves; the shepherd simply brings them to the good food. Sheep are ruminant animals, and they spend a large part of the day grazing and chewing their cud.

We are to spiritually feed ourselves daily. Jesus is our daily bread, and we will grow weak and hungry if we do not dig into Him. Simply letting Sunday morning church or Wednesday Bible study feed us will leave us hungry and weak. We need to daily digest the things of our Savior. We also need to return to the good things we have already learned or are in the process of learning. Chew on the things the Shepherd is revealing, ruminant on His character that He is making known.

Sheep learn the voice of the shepherd and will only follow their shepherd. Sheep will respond only to the voice they know and trust, even when they hear other voices. A shepherd who knows his sheep knows that the sheep of his flock will come when he calls.

Every day, there are voices calling for your attention. We are sheep and we will be following a shepherd's voice—Make sure the voice you follow is Jesus. Every morning, you will hear things calling for your attention—fear, lies, your past, and sin raging among them. But better than all these is the voice of Jesus, always calling out to you. Knowing His voice is so important. Learn His words and only follow Him. The Good Shepherd longs for His sheep to know Him and to walk with Him in a deeply intimate relationship.

Sheep have a remarkably high pain tolerance, which means that a shepherd must be extremely watchful and vigilant. Sheep will not show obvious signs of sickness until it has reached a critical level, and at that point, the sheep needs immediate attention or it will die within a few days. Because of this, shepherds must have an extremely intimate knowledge of their sheep, more so than with any other species. A good shepherd will be able to detect illness in his sheep early and be able to prevent sickness from becoming critical.

We are often good at hiding issues until they reach critical levels. Jesus knows us so intimately however that He knows the instant we are affected by something, long before we may even realize it ourselves. We need a lot of attention, but this isn't a bad thing. Our Good Shepherd knows we need Him, for He designed us this way. He detects things in us before we even know they're there, and He is with us every moment to give us everything we could ever need, and so much more.

> So he told them this parable: "What man of you, having a hundred sheep, if he has lost one of them, does not leave the ninety-nine in the open country, and go after the one that is lost, until he finds it? And when he has found it, he lays it on his shoulders, rejoicing. And when he comes home, he calls together his friends and his neighbors, saying to them, 'Rejoice with me, for I have found my sheep that was lost.' Just so, I tell you, there will be more joy in heaven over one sinner who repents than over ninety-nine righteous persons who need no repentance." (Luke 15:3–7)

There are breeds of sheep that are extremely gregarious, which is the instinct for them to stay in large groups. These breeds rarely wonder away from the group in numbers less than 20 to 30. This allows them to be managed, moved, and maintained without fences and is how the range operations function.

In this setting, shepherds need to be able to account for all of their sheep, and to be able to count them quickly, there would often be black sheep spread throughout the flock. The shepherd would then count the black sheep among the white, and if a black sheep was missing, it would be an indicator that a larger number was gone, and the shepherd could then turn back or send someone for them accordingly.

In the parable of the lost sheep, there are 100 sheep. The Shepherd looks out and sees that 1 is missing. He knows His flock so well that He can instantly tell that a single sheep is not among the rest. In large operations, looking for 1 sheep is not worth the effort or potential danger that such a task would lead to. However, the Good Shepherd misses the 1 and goes off searching to bring His sheep home. The Shepherd trusts the 99 enough to know that they will wait for Him as He brings the 1 home. It is truly remarkable that the Shepherd notices the missing sheep and our worth is screamed out as He goes and finds His lost sheep.

We have all been the 1 sheep, and most of us have probably been one of the 99. Jesus boldly loves both. He is our Good Shepherd. He anticipates our needs and even designed us so that the depths of our lives will be fulfilled in Him. He heals us and attends to us daily, and He invites us deeper still.

> Truly, truly, I tell you, whoever does not enter the sheepfold by the gate, but climbs in some other way, is a thief and a robber. But the one who enters by the gate is the shepherd of the sheep. The gatekeeper opens the gate for him, and the sheep listen for his voice. He calls his own sheep by name and leads them out. When he has brought out all who are his own, he goes on ahead of them, and his sheep follow him because they know his voice. But they will never follow a stranger; in fact, they will flee from him because they do not recognize his voice.
>
> Jesus spoke to them using this illustration, but they did not understand what He was telling them. So He said to them again, "Truly, truly, I tell you, I am the gate for the sheep. All who came before Me were thieves and robbers, but the

sheep did not listen to them. I am the gate. If anyone enters through Me, he will be saved. He will come in and go out and find pasture." (John 10:1–9; Berean Study Bible)

The sheepfold was where the shepherds and sheep would find sanctuary at night. A sheepfold was a paddock made of stone with only one opening for the entrance. There was no gate on the sheepfold, so a shepherd would lie down in the open gap and become the gate for the night. The shepherd would be between the sheep and anything that would mean them harm. Jesus is our Good Shepherd who stands in the gap and is the gate.

Enter through the narrow gate. For wide is the gate and broad is the road that leads to destruction, and many enter through it. (Matthew 7:13; NIV)

The narrow gate isn't found tucked into a mountain with a dangerous, rocky, and steep road leading to it. The narrow gate isn't hidden. Jesus is the gate. Entering through the narrow gate means walking into His sheepfold and being a part of His flock. He is our Good Shepherd; and He longs for us, His sheep, to know His voice. Being His sheep means that we follow Him, knowing that He will provide every measure of protection, guidance, and anything else we need.

And he said to his disciples, "Therefore I tell you, do not be anxious about your life, what you will eat, nor about your body, what you will put on. For life is more than food, and the body more than clothing. Consider the ravens: they neither sow nor reap, they have neither storehouse nor barn, and yet God feeds them. Of how much more value are you than the birds! And which of you by being anxious can add a single hour to his span of life? If then you are not able to do as small a thing as that, why are you anxious about the rest? Consider the lilies, how they grow: they neither toil nor spin, yet I tell you, even Solomon in all his glory was not arrayed like one of these. But if God so clothes the grass, which is alive in the field today, and tomorrow is thrown into the over, how much more will he clothe you, o you of little faith! And do not seek what you are to eat and what you are to drink, nor be worried. For all the nations of the world seek after these things, and your Father knows that you need them. Instead, seek his kingdom, and these things will be added to you.

"Fear not, little flock, for it is your Father's good pleasure to give you the kingdom. Sell your possessions, and give to the needy. Provide yourselves with moneybags that do not grow old, with a treasure in the heavens that does not fail, where no thief approaches and no moth destroys. For where your treasure is, there will your heart be also." (Luke 12:34)

"Fear not, little flock, for it is your Father's good pleasure to give you the kingdom." Entering through the narrow gate is the entrance into the Kingdom. We have a life to live as a part of His flock. Sometimes we are satisfied with only remembering that Jesus died for our sin. Our salvation is incredibly important, and we need to take time to understand the measure to which Christ took our place on the cross. We need time to heal and truly know who Grace is, because you can't impart something that you don't possess.

But even greater than the death of Christ is that He rose again! Stopping at salvation isn't incorrect; it's incomplete.[2]

Salvation is our entrance into the Kingdom of Heaven. Christ's death was our salvation and set us up to be fit for the Kingdom. Christ's resurrection was the bold declaration that the Kingdom is on this earth now, and our signal to march forward into the greater things that Jesus already won for us.

Jesus shows us that the Kingdom is today by the life He lived. If our focus was to be only on our salvation, Jesus would have focused more on our sin and shame. But Jesus loved relentlessly, healed every sickness He was in contact with and took away every measure of shame. Jesus showed us how we are to boldly live in His Kingdom and how we can release more of His reign onto this earth. Our world is out of order, but we live in the Kingdom that has the power to begin setting things back into their original design.

The message that Jesus taught to the masses was not that He was going to be dying in their place. The cross was His means of releasing us into His Kingdom. The Good News of the Gospel is this:

> Repent, for the Kingdom of Heaven has come near. (Matthew 3:2)

The Kingdom is on earth today. Jesus taught us Kingdom principles and showed us what life looks like when we are active members of the Kingdom of Heaven. Let's follow Him today as we walk deeper into the abundant life that Jesus has won for us.

> *Jesus, thank You for being our Good Shepherd. Thank You for allowing us to hear Your voice and be able to follow You. Thank You Jesus for standing in the gap for us. Thank You for being our entrance into Your Kingdom. Teach us to only hear Your voice and to make You our Good Shepherd. Thank You for providing everything for us, and may we rest in the truth of who You are. Jesus, walk us into Your Kingdom and show us how to live a life that daily brings Heaven to earth.*

Chapter 18

EDEN

The Garden of Eden was designed as the dwelling place for God and man. This oasis was God's original intent for life on earth. The Lord God formed man and then placed him into the garden.[1] Genesis 1 and 2 contain the beautiful account of the creation story. These descriptions are not a timeline of how the earth was created, but a poetic description of God forming life on this earth. This place He designed was made so that we could dwell in His presence, and we long for this home.

The most remarkable part about Eden is that God was with man. The original design was for God to walk with His creation.

> And they heard the sound of the Lord God
> walking in the garden in the cool of the day.
> (Genesis 3:8a)

This sentence usually goes unnoticed because the response is that Adam and Eve hide from God, and we are focused on their sin and the fall of man. But we must realize the significance of what this is saying. Adam and Eve did not see God in the garden, but they knew it was Him by the sound of His approach. They recognized the sound because they heard it often. Every evening, in the cool of the day, the Lord God walked with man in the garden.

This was our Lord God's intent with creation. He told us we could eat of every tree, except one.[2] He wants us to have what we like. He made an entire garden of different types of fruit and told us to eat what tasted best to us. He blessed us before we did anything.[3] Our Creator's intent for life was an intimate garden where we do what we love and are always in His presence.

The serpent convinces Adam and Eve that the Lord is keeping something from them. Throughout Genesis, the Father is named as the Lord God; but when the serpent is trying to instill sin, he refers to the Creator as God. By calling Him God instead of the Lord God, the serpent undermines the relationship that the Father has established with man. Adam and Eve believe lies that the Father is keeping good things from them and that the relationship is tainted. Because they believe lies, they sin and are forced out of Eden because our good God cannot be partnered with sin.

We know that God's original intent for this earth is still His end goal for us. He is leading us back into a home where we may forever dwell with Him.

> Then I saw a new heaven and a new earth, for the first heaven and the first earth had passed away, and the sea was no more. And I saw the holy city, new Jerusalem, coming down out of heaven from God, prepared as a bride adorned for her husband. And I heard a loud voice from the throne saying, "Behold, the dwelling place of God is with man. He will dwell with them, and they will be his people, and God himself will be with them as their God. He will wipe away every tear from their eyes, and death shall be no more, neither shall there be mourning, nor crying, nor pain anymore, for the former things have passed away." (Revelation 21:1–4)

> And I saw no temple in the city, for its temple is the Lord God the Almighty and the Lamb.

And the city has no need of sun or moon to shine on it, for the glory of God gives it light, and its lamp is the Lamb. By its light will the nations walk, and the kings of the earth will bring their glory into it, and its gates will never be shut by day – and there will be no night there. They will bring into it the glory and the honor of the nations. But nothing unclean will ever enter it, nor anyone who does what is detestable or false, but only those who are written in the Lamb's book of life. (Revelation 21:22–27)

Then the angel showed me the river of the water of life, bright as crystal, flowing from the throne of God and of the Lamb through the middle of the street of the city; also, on either side of the river, the tree of life with its twelve kinds of fruit, yielding its fruit each month. The leaves of the tree were for the healing of the nations. No longer will there be anything accursed, but the throne of God and of the Lamb will be in it, and his servants will worship him. They will see his face, and his name will be on their foreheads. And night will be no more. They will need no light of lamp or sun, for the Lord God will be their light, and they will reign forever and ever. (Revelation 22:1–5)

The descriptions we get of our new home sounds like a garden city, maybe even the garden we read about in Genesis. Wherever the place may be, the intent is very clear. The Lord God is bringing us to a place where we may dwell with Him, for He longs to be with us. Ever since the fall, our Lord God has been working to get us back to the Garden of Eden. The entire Old Testament is our redemption story.

After Adam and Eve sinned, they had to leave the garden. Many years go by and eventually, we end up in Exodus, with Moses and the Israelites living in tents in the desert. It is here that the Lord instructs Moses to build the tabernacle. Later, in 2 Samuel, King David makes plans to build a temple. This temple is then constructed by King Solomon, the son of David, of which the Lord said:

> Now the word of the Lord came to Solomon, "Concerning this house that you are building, if you will walk in my statutes and obey my rules and keep all my commandments and walk in them, then I will establish my word with you, which I spoke to David your father. And I will dwell among the children of Israel and will not forsake my people Israel." (1 King 6:11–13)

The Lord calls the temple a house, for it is His house. The tabernacle and the temple have the same layout and serve the same purpose—They house the Presence of the Lord.

The tabernacle, and later the temple, had an outer court that was for worshippers. This court was surrounding a building that held the Holy Place and the Holy of Holies. Only priests were allowed in the Holy Place, and only the High Priest was allowed in the Holy of Holies, which was right behind the Holy Place. Separating these two rooms was a large, heavy curtain that hung from ceiling to floor. And behind it, in the Holy of Holies, was where the presence of the Lord dwelled.

The role of the High Priest was to prepare for the Day of Atonement. The High Priest would spend all year doing rituals in order to prepare for this day. The Day of Atonement was designed to take all of Israel's sins before the Lord and offer sacrifices. Once a year, the High Priest would go behind the veil and offer sacrifices to the Lord.

Before going into the Holy of Holies, a rope was tied around the High Priest and he was given a bell. As he moved into the presence of the Lord, the priest would ring his bell. And if the bell stopped ringing, the priests would use the rope to retrieve the body of the now deceased High Priest. And more often than not, the High Priest would die, and there would be another year of preparation before another High Priest could go before the Lord and offer sacrifices on behalf of all the people of Israel.

The reason the High Priest would often die when he came into the presence of the Lord was because if he had not performed all the proper rituals perfectly and was not completely in step within the law, he would not be able to live in the presence of the Lord. This is not because God would smite him, but it was because sin cannot stand before the Lord. Sin cannot stand when brought into the glory of the Creator. This is why Adam and Eve had to leave the garden, not because God was being mean to them, but because if they stayed, they would surely die. This is the extent to which our sin had separated us from the Father.

With the tabernacle, the Lord is able to dwell with His people for the first time since Eden. God's people were living in tents, and so He decided He would as well. And when God's people moved into a permanent structure, God did as well and the temple was constructed. And now, our Lord dwells with us in an even more extraordinary way.

> And Jesus cried out again and with a loud voice and yielded up his spirit.
>
> And behold, the curtain of the temple was torn in two, from top to bottom. And the earth shook, and the rocks were split. The tombs also were opened. And many bodies of the saints who had fallen asleep were raised, and coming out of the tombs after his resurrection they went into the holy city and appeared to many. When the centurion and those who were with him, keeping watch over Jesus, saw the earthquake and what took place, they were filled with awe and said, "Truly this was the Son of God!" (Matthew 27:50–54)

At the moment of Christ's death, the curtain in the temple was torn from top to bottom. Jesus, the perfect Lamb, was sacrificed as our sin. This fulfilled the law and released the Spirit of the Lord into all the earth. No longer must He be contained behind a curtain, for we are washed in the blood of the Lamb. The curtain is torn and the earth shook, rocks crumbled, and the dead raised! Never again will we be separated from the presence of our Lord, Jesus has done it, and it is finished.

And there's more! In Acts 2, pillars of fire fall onto the apostles as they are filled with the Holy Spirit. Not only does the presence of the Lord dwell on earth, but the very Spirit that raised Jesus from the grave now lives in us.

> Do you not know that you are God's temple and that God's Spirit dwells in you? (1 Corinthians 3:16)

We have become the temple because the presence of the Lord has been placed in our hearts. We are sealed with the Holy Spirit. You have become the house of the Lord. Walk with the understanding of what is within you.

> Are you tired? Worn out? Burned out on religion? Come to me. Get away with me and you'll recover your life. I'll show you how to take a real rest. Walk with me and work with me – watch how I do it. Learn the unforced rhythms of grace. I won't lay anything heavy or ill-fitting on you. Keep company with me and you'll learn to live freely and lightly. (Matthew 11:28–30; MSG)

Jesus invites us to walk with Him, and because of the Holy Spirit, we are able to daily walk side by side with our Savior. Our sin once distanced us from our Father. This distance caused distortion in our understanding of Him and the life He has in mind for us.

Distortion is overcome with communication. And we have overcome our distorted image of the Father through the communication we now experience with Him through the Spirit that is within us. Jesus came and revealed the Father's heart to us, released us from sin, and now invites us to once again walk with Him just as we once did in Eden.

Eden can be defined as the place where God and His people dwell. And this is how the Kingdom of Heaven has come near. This is how the Kingdom is moving on this earth. The Kingdom is alive and active because the Spirit of God is within us.

Walk with the knowledge of what lies within you. Start to operate in the power that is already there. You become unstoppable when you set your mind onto the things of the Kingdom.

> *Papa, thank You for Eden. Thank You for longing to dwell with us. Thank You for removing everything that stood in the way of this. You are so good and kind and we long for more of You. Teach us to cultivate Your presence. Place a burning desire in our hearts to dwell today in Your presence and love and goodness. May we glorify Your name every day. Jesus, lead us deeper into Your Kingdom. Teach us how to dwell in You more deeply and allow us to show the world who You are. Help us always be aware of the Spirit in us, and teach us to let Your Spirit move freely in our hearts and through our lives.*

Chapter 19

ISRAEL

The Kingdom belongs to God's people. In the Old Testament, Israel is named as God's chosen people. This made many people believe that God wanted only these people, and people thought that it was their nationality or position in life that makes them belong to God.

However, chosen does not mean favorite. All people belong to God. Jesus came and died for all sin because He longs for all people to come to Him. Jesus constantly spent time with the outcasts of society rather than the elites. God longs for all people—all nations. There is no exception from who God wants as His.

He chose Israel to be the agents to make His glory known. He set aside Israel as His remnant warriors. He chose them to stay loyal and to stay on task. God chose Israel to be a people that would show the world the love of the Father and to bring worshippers home.

Israel was blessed to be a blessing. They were shown favor so that the Lord's goodness would be known and that all people could see the kindness that the Lord showed to those who are His. Their blessings were to be used to bless the people around them and to create in everyone a longing to know a God who was good and kind.

Now the Lord God said to Abram, "Go
from your country and your kindred and your

father's house to the land that I will show you. And I will make of you a great nation, and I will bless you and make your name great, so that you will be a blessing. I will bless those who bless you, and him who dishonors you I will curse, and in you all the families of the earth shall be blessed." (Genesis 12:1–3)

Abraham went out to begin to make a people for God. Israel was chosen so that they could co-labor with God, and now, the Church today continues the work of Israel as we co-labor with Jesus. The chosen Israel began the work that the chosen Bride of Christ now continues. The Church is the Bride of Christ, and we work today for the same task that was given to Israel.

The Israelites spent 400 years in slavery in Egypt. They cried out to God but were not released from their oppression for 400 years. They spent this time growing in numbers, and when Moses was finally appointed to lead His people out, Israel had grown into a great nation. They leave for the Promised Land with a purpose to win the world for God, but they struggle. Their hearts are hardened and they rebel. God redeems His people over and over again as they continue to fall short of being the people He called them to be.

There were 400 years of silence before John the Baptist began his work. John prepares the way for Jesus. Jesus came and did what we could never do and set us up to be able to complete the task that has been assigned since the beginning. The apostles start the Church, which is a continuation of the work of Israel. Jews are the Israelites from the tribe of Judah; and so as the Church begins, they go mostly to Jews, still keeping the message within Israel. But in the Book of Acts, this starts to change.

> Now those who were scattered because of the persecution that arose over Stephen traveled as far as Phoenicia and Cyprus and Antioch, speaking the word to no one except Jews. But there were some of them, men of Cyprus and

Cyrene, who on coming to Antioch spoke to the Hellenists also, preaching the Lord Jesus. And the hand of the Lord was with them, and a great number who believed turned to the Lord. The report of this came to the ears of the church in Jerusalem, and they sent Barnabas to Antioch. When he came and saw the grace of God, he was glad, and he exhorted them all to remain faithful to the Lord with steadfast purpose, for he was a good man, full of the Holy Spirit and of faith. And a great many people were added to the Lord. So Barnabas went to Tarsus to look for Saul, and when he had found him, he brought him to Antioch. For a whole year they met with the church and taught a great many people. And in Antioch the disciples were first called Christians. (Acts 11:19–26)

They call themselves Christians because God is no longer moving only through the Jewish people, the Israelites. In Acts 15, the Holy Spirit falls on the Gentiles, just as it had fallen on the Jews in Acts 2. People no longer have to convert to Judaism to know God. They name themselves Christians because Jesus is for all people, nations, and cultures and no longer is He confined to one people group. God is glorified more fully when people praise Him in their own culture. The Church is open to all people because Jesus made the way for every person to come as they are.

The Church is now Israel. But the church is not just a building just as Israel was not just a nation. The Church is the people of God. The Church is the people who have been chosen for a specific purpose. And we are now empowered by the work of Jesus and the gift of the Holy Spirit to see the completion of the task that God's people have been working for since the beginning.

God is seeking for Himself people who will worship Him with a pure heart. He is a rightly jealous lover, for He is the only thing worthy of our praise. The Great Commission is not a new task. The command to make disciples for God is seen throughout the entire Bible.

> And the angel of the Lord called to Abraham a second time from heaven and said, "By myself I have sworn, declares the Lord, because you have done this and have not withheld your son, your only son, **I will surely bless you, and I will surely multiply your offspring as the stars of heaven and as the sand that is on the seashore.** And your offspring shall possess the gate of his enemies, **and in your offspring shall all the nations of the earth be blessed**, because you have obeyed my voice." (Genesis 22:15–18)

> Your offspring shall be like the dust of the earth, **and you shall spread abroad** to the west and to the east and to the north and to the south, **and in you and your offspring shall all the families of the earth be blessed**. (Genesis 28:14)

> Then the Lord said to Moses, "Rise up early in the morning and present yourself before Pharaoh and say to him, 'Thus says the Lord, the God of the Hebrews, "Let my people go, that they may serve me. For this time I will send all my plagues on you yourself, and on your servants and your people, **so that you may know that there in none like me in all the earth**. For by now I could have put out my hand and stuck you and your people with pestilence, and you would have been cut off from the earth. But for this purpose I have raised you up, to show you my power, **so that my name may be proclaimed in all the earth.** (Exodus 9:13–16)

See, I have taught you statutes and rules, as the Lord my God commanded me, that you should do them in the land that you are entering to take possession of it. Keep them and do them, for that will be your wisdom and your understanding in the sight of the peoples, who, when they hear all these statues, will say, "Surely this great nation is a wise and understanding people." **For what great nation is there that has a god so near to it as the Lord our God is to us, whenever we call upon him?** (Deuteronomy 4:5–7)

And you [God] saw the affliction of our fathers in Egypt and heard their cry at the Red Sea, and performed signs and wonders against Pharaoh and all his servants and all the people of his land, for you knew that they acted arrogantly against our fathers. **And you made a name for yourself, as it is to this day.** (Nehemiah 9:9–10)

For the Lord your God dried up the waters of the Jordan for you until you passed over, as the Lord your God did to the Red Sea, which he dried up for us until we passed over, **so that all the people of the earth may know that the hand of the Lord is mighty, that you may fear the Lord you God forever.** (Joshua 4:23–24)

For this I will praise you, O Lord, **among the nations**, and sing praises to your name. (2 Samuel 22:50)

Likewise, when a foreigner, who is not of your people Israel, comes from a far country for you name's sake (for they shall hear of your great name and your mighty hand, and of your outstretched arm), when he comes and prays toward this house, hear in heaven your dwelling place and do according to all for which the foreigner calls to you, **in order that all the peoples of the earth may know your name and fear you**, as do your people Israel, **and that they may know that this house that I have built is called by your name**. (1 King 8:41–43)

Be still, and know that I am God. **I will be exalted among the nations, I will be exalted in the earth!** (Psalm 46:10)

May God be gracious to us **and bless us and make his face to shine upon us**, Selah, **that your way may be known on earth, your saving power among all nations.** Let the peoples praise you, O God; let all the peoples praise you! **Let the nations be glad and sing for joy**, for you judge the peoples with equity and guide the nations upon earth. Selah. **Let the peoples praise you, O God; let all the peoples praise you!** The earth has yielded its increase; **God, our God, shall bless us. God shall bless us; let all the ends of the earth fear him!** (Psalm 67)

You are the God who works wonders; **you have made known your might among the peoples.** (Psalm 77:14)

He says: "It is too light a thing that you should be my servant to raise up the tries of Jacob and to bring back the preserved of Israel; **I will make you as a light for the nations, that my salvation may reach to the end of the earth.**" (Isaiah 49:6)

If you return, O Israel, declares the Lord, to me you should return. If you remove your detestable things from my presence, and do not waver, and if you swear, "As the Lord lives," in truth, in justice, and in righteousness, **then nations shall bless themselves in Him, and in Him shall they glory.** (Jeremiah 4:1–2)

For the earth will be filled with the knowledge of the glory of the Lord as the waters cover the sea. (Habakkuk 2:14)

God has worked from the very beginning to set Himself apart from all others. He has made His name known to all nations through His glorious might and power. He keeps favor on His people to draw everyone to Himself. He blesses us and cherishes us in ways that we will never stop discovering. His heart is clear in the Old Testament, and Jesus came to reveal it more fully.

Now there was a man in Jerusalem, whose name was Simeon, and this man was righteous and devout, waiting for the consolation of Israel, and the Holy Spirit was upon him. And it had been revealed to him by the Holy Spirit that he would not see death before he had seen the Lord's Christ. And he came in the Spirit into the temple, and when the parents brought in the child Jesus, to do for him according to the custom of the Law, he took him up in his arms and blessed God and said, "Lord, now you are letting your servant depart in peace, according to your word; for my eyes have seen your salvation that you have prepared in the presence of all the peoples, **a light for revelation to the Gentiles, and for glory to your people Israel.**" (Luke 2:25–32)

Now the eleven disciples went to Galilee, to the mountain to which Jesus had directed them. And when they saw him they worshiped him, but some doubted. And Jesus came and said to them, "All authority in heaven and on earth has been given to me. Go therefore and **make disciples of all nations**, baptizing them in the name of the Father and of the Son and of the Holy Spirit, teaching them to observe all that I have commanded you. And behold, I am with you always, to the ends of the age." (Matthew 28:16–20)

So then the Lord Jesus, after he had spoken to them, was taken up into heaven and sat down at the right hand of God. **And they went out and preached everywhere**, while the Lord worked with them and confirmed the message by accompanying signs. (Mark 16:19–20)

But you will receive power when the Holy Spirit has come upon you, and you will be my witnesses **in Jerusalem and in all Judea and Samaria, and to the ends of the earth**. (Acts 1:8)

And all the prophets who have spoken, from Samuel and those who came after him, also proclaimed these days. You are the sons of the prophets and of the covenant that God made with your fathers, saying to Abraham, **"And in your offspring shall all the families of the earth be blessed."** (Acts 3:24–25)

For so the Lord commanded us, saying, **"I have made you a light for the Gentiles, that you may bring salvation to the ends of the earth."** (Acts 13:47)

And they sang a new song, saying, "Worthy are you to take the scroll and to open its seals, for you were slain, and by your blood **you ransomed people for God from every tribe and language and people and nation**, and you have made them a kingdom and priests to our God, and they shall reign on the earth." (Revelations 5:9–10)

After this I looked, and behold, **a great multitude** that no one could number, **from every nation, from all tribes and peoples and languages,** standing before the throne and before the Lamb, clothed in white robes, with palm branches in their hands, and crying out with a loud voice, "Salvation belongs to our God who sits on the throne, and to the Lamb!" (Revelations 7:9–10)[1]

Can you see the themes woven into our story? We are given two very clear commands. Our Lord says to us, "Enjoy my grace, and extend my glory."[2]

Enjoy His Grace! Time and time again, He blesses us. He delights in giving us what we desire. He is a good Father, and He longs to give us good gifts.

Extend His glory! Our God is the one true God. He has worked hard to make His name and might known, and we are to partner with Him in this. Our Father longs for every single person to know Him. He is a missionary God and will stop at nothing to get His children home.

As a Christian, as one who believes that Jesus Christ is Lord, you are chosen by God. You are chosen to enjoy His grace and to extend His glory. Help the world taste and see that He is good, just as you have.

We have been given a task. Our mission is to tell all people about our Lord. And it's not just about knowing facts about Him. Our Lord God longs to be in deep and intimate relationship with His people. We are to know God and be known by God, and nothing on this earth is greater than this. He has made the way clear for us, because through Jesus, we are made righteous, holy, and redeemed. We are clean and pure and are able to boldly approach His throne. We never have to leave His Grace, for His Spirit is within us, and surely He will be with us always.

If you confess that Jesus Christ is the Son of God and that He has died and risen, then this is your mission. You are a Kingdom member and you are to daily enjoy His grace and extend His glory.

> *Papa, thank You for revealing to us Your heart. Thank You for being a missionary God who goes to great lengths to bring people to Yourself. Thank You for calling to us first, for we would not call to You if You had not first been calling to us. Help us to clearly see the things You have set before us. May we step into the mission that You have called us to do. Teach us how to enjoy Your grace and to extend Your glory. We long to be the people who can complete the task that You have given us from the beginning. Give us Your heart for the nations. May the Lamb that was slain receive the reward for His suffering.*

Oh sing to the Lord a new song;
sing to the Lord, all the earth!
Sing to the Lord, bless his name;
tell of his salvation from day to day.
Declare his glory among the nations,
his marvelous works among all the peoples!
For great is the Lord, and greatly to be praised;
he is to be feared above all gods,
For all the gods of the peoples are worthless idols,
but the Lord made the heavens.
Splendor and majesty are before him;
strength and beauty are in his sanctuary.
Ascribe to the Lord, O families of the peoples,
ascribe to the Lord glory and strength!

KINGDOM COME

Ascribe to the Lord the glory due his name;
bring an offering, and come into his courts!
Worship the Lord in the splendor of holiness;
tremble before him, all the earth!
Say among the nations, "The Lord reigns!
Yes, the world is established; it shall never be moved;
he will judge the peoples with equity."
Let the heavens be glad, and let the earth rejoice;
let the sea roar, and all that fills it;
let the field exult, and everything in it!
Then shall all the trees of the forest sing for joy
before the Lord, for he comes,
for he comes to judge the earth.
He will judge the world in righteousness,
and the peoples in his faithfulness. (Psalm 96)

Chapter 20

FLIPPING TABLES

> And Jesus entered the temple and drove out all who sold and bought in the temple, and he overturned tables of the money-changers and the seats of those who sold pigeons. He said to them, "It is written, 'My house shall be called a house of prayer,' but you make it a den of robbers."
>
> And the blind and the lame came to him in the temple, and he healed them. (Matthew 21:12–14)

Jesus is consumed with righteous anger when He sees how the temple has been treated. People have set up shop to make a profit off of those coming to worship the Lord. This entire court must have been filled with commotion as it had become a marketplace. This would have been a huge hindrance on any person looking to pray.

What's more, the court that they had taken over was the court for the Gentiles. Jews set up shop in a court designed for the people of different nations to come to the Lord.

> And he was teaching them and saying to them, "Is it not written, 'My house shall be called

a house of prayer for all the nations?' But you
have made it a den of robbers." (Mark 11:17)

Our Father is for all people—all nations. The original design for
the temple didn't even have a separate court for Gentile worshipers,
but the Jews added one and so put more barriers between people and
God.

Jesus calls what the court had become a den of robbers, not
because they were doing unfair business but because they were rob-
bing people from their time of prayer and worship in the house of
the Lord.

Jesus flips the tables. Jesus spent His entire ministry removing
anything that kept us from our Father. Jesus goes into His Father's
house and cleanses it, removing everything that kept people from
worshiping within the temple.

And then Jesus moves outward. Not only does He cleanse the
temple on the inside and make it pure, He also then goes out and
brings the right thing to fill it.

Jesus stood outside the temple and the masses came to Him—
the blind, the lame, and any who needed healing. And Jesus healed
them all, Jew and Gentile. For the first time, these once sick people
are able to go into the temple, because before they were considered
unclean due to their sickness and could not enter.

Jesus went out and filled the temple with what it was designed
to hold—the people of God. He removed every barrier that hindered
anyone from praying and worshiping in the house of the Lord.

Jesus flipped tables everywhere He went. He removed every barrier that once kept us away from our Father and we are now free to
boldly approach His throne.

We were once dead in our sin, and now we are dead to our sin.
We were separated from the Father so Jesus flipped tables to change
this.

Or do you not know, brothers – for I am
speaking to those who know the law – that the
law is binding on a person only as long as he lives?

> For a married woman is bound by law to her husband while he lives, but if her husband dies she is released from the law of marriage. Accordingly, she will be called an adulteress if she lives with another man while her husband is alive. But if her husband dies, she is free from that law, and if she marries another man she is not an adulteress.
>
> Likewise, my brothers, you also have died to the law through the body of Christ, so that you may belong to another, to him who has been raised from the dead, in order that we may bear fruit for God. For while we were living in the flesh, our sinful passions, aroused by the law, were at work in our members to bear fruit for death. But now we are released from the law, having died to that which held us captive, so that we serve in the new way of the Spirit and not in the old way of the written code. (Romans 7:1–6)

Understand the extent to which you were dead in your sin. If you broke even a single rule, you were guilty of breaking the entire law. Therefore, we all had fallen short of the law and were guilty on all accounts. But Jesus came and fulfilled the law and now we are betrothed to another.

> For I feel a divine jealousy for you, since I betrothed you to one husband, to present you as a pure virgin to Christ. (2 Corinthians 11:2)

Jesus flipped over and completely did away with the tables of our sin. He cannot stand to have things stand in the way of us being with Him, and He continues to flip things around when there is opposition to His purpose.

The time period that Jesus was on earth was truly a blessed time. It was during the Pax Romana, meaning there was peace in the Roman Empire and because of this, the Gospel message had the means to travel throughout the known world. We know that the message was for every people, and we can see how serious our God is about that.

The Last Supper took place during Passover, which is a Jewish holiday; and as tradition, the Jews would gather and stay for 50 days until Pentecost. In this 50-day time period, there was a large number of Jews from all around in Jerusalem.[1]

After He is resurrected, Jesus spends 40 days walking the earth, revealing Himself to people and teaching.[2] After 40 days, He ascends into Heaven and sends His disciples to the city to wait for Him. And on the day of Pentecost, the apostles are filled with the Holy Spirit and go out speaking all different languages, and the Jews from all around who had gathered would have heard the message that Peter delivers. This was at the end of their 50-day-long visit to Jerusalem, and they would go home carrying this new salvation with them. The Good News gets an immediate kick-start this way as our Father had already orchestrated that there would be a mass gathering in Jerusalem ripe to accept and carry home the Gospel message.

As the message is spread and the Church multiplies, Jesus leaves us with a commandment.

> But you will receive power when the Holy Spirit has come upon you, and you will be my witnesses in Jerusalem and in all Judea and Samaria, and to the ends of the earth. (Acts 1:8)

We read in Acts that after this, there was an amount of time that the new Christians stayed in Jerusalem, not obeying the command to carry the message throughout the earth. But, Jesus had a plan.

> And there arose on that day a great persecution against the church in Jerusalem, and they were all scattered throughout the regions of Judea and Samaria, except the apostles. (Acts 8:1)

This persecution was used as a way to get the message out of the city of Jerusalem. When we are given commands such as Acts 1:8, we will encounter experiences like Acts 8:1 in order to accomplish the works that we have been assigned.

We are to be fruitful and multiply, and Jesus will flip any and every table that gets in the way of the Good News being spread throughout the entire earth. Jesus is serious about the task He was given, and we should be too. Just as Jesus flipped tables, we are to join Him in breaking down barriers between God and His people.

We are to be flipping tables, but sometimes, we get caught up chasing coat tails.

> As Jesus went, the people pressed around him. And there was a woman who had had a discharge of blood for twelve years, and though she had spent all her living on physicians, she could not be healed by anyone. She came up behind him and touched the fringe of his garment, and immediately her discharge of blood ceased. And Jesus said, "Who was it that touched me?" When all denied it, Peter said, "Master, the crowds surround you and are pressing in on you!" But Jesus said, "Someone touched me, for I perceive that power has gone out from me." And when the woman saw that she was not hidden, she came trembling, and falling down before him declared in the presence of all the people why she had touched him, and how she had been immediately healed. And he said to her, "Daughter, your faith has made you well; go in peace." (Luke 8:42–48)

And why was this woman trying to touch Jesus?

> For she said to herself, "If I only touch his garment, I will be made well." (Matthew 9:21)

Sometimes, we reach out to touch the fringes of Jesus just to become well. We look for a quick fix to our issues and long for only a touch. But Jesus is not okay with only healing us. He stops and turns around and gives the nameless woman a voice and a story. And not only that, He restores her into the right relationship with Him along with her newly healed body. How often do we reach out for only a touch when He is desiring a deep connection. He has already flipped the tables, so now we just come to Him. We don't chase the fringes of His coat tails, for He turns around and looks right at us.

Since we no longer only reach for the fringes, we can begin flipping tables for other people. Because Jesus has fixed His gaze on us, we are able to start directing our attention at those around us.

> Now Peter and John were going up to the temple at the hour of prayer, the ninth hour. And a man lame from birth was being carried, whom they laid daily at the gate of the temple that is called the Beautiful Gate to ask alms of those entering the temple. Seeing Peter and John about to go into the temple, he asked to receive alms. And Peter directed his gaze at him, as did John, and said, "Look at us." And he fixed his attention on them, expecting to receive something from them. But Peter said, "I have no silver and gold, but what I do have I give to you. In the name of Jesus Christ of Nazareth, rise up and walk!" And he took him by the right hand and raised him up, and immediately his feet and ankles were made strong. And leaping up he stood and began to walk, and entered the temple with them, walking and leaping and praising God. And all the people saw him walking and praising God, and recognized him as the one who sat at the Beautiful Gate of the temple, asking for alms. And they were filled with wonder and amazement at what had happened to him. (Acts 3:1–10)

Every day, this man was carried to the gate to beg. He would get enough money for food, be taken home, and then be brought the next day to do it again. He had never walked, let alone step foot into the temple.

Jesus's disciples walk by and see him and probably know his story. He's asking for little, but what they give him is life. They command his attention in order to get him to stop looking at the world and for him to begin to focus of Jesus. He is healed by a word and his life is changed.

How often does this world ask for little—just to get by, just to make it to tomorrow, just to stop hurting? And we walk around with life giving words that can change everything. Flip tables so that all may go into the presence of the Lord singing and dancing and walking for the first time. We bring people water, and Jesus makes it wine.[3]

Jesus was a table-flipper and so are you.

> *Jesus, thank You for flipping tables. Thank You for removing every single barrier between us and the Father. Thank You for fulfilling the law and allowing us to boldly approach the throne. You are good and kind and faithful, and we give everything to You. Teach us to flip tables in our own lives; teach us to immediately remove anything in the way of our relationship with You. And more than that, teach us how to flip tables for the people around us. Show us the things that are in the way of people knowing You, and may we be a Church that removes every barrier.*

Chapter 21

STATUS REPORT

So we know the task we were given. And we can rejoice because we are not joining a dying fight. We know the outcome we are heading towards, and for the first time, we are living in a generation that can see the complete of our task.

> Truly, truly, I say to you, whoever believes in me will also do the works that I do; and greater works than these will he do, because I am going to the Father. Whatever you ask in my name, this I will do, that the Father may be glorified in the Son. If you ask me anything in my name, I will do it. (John 14:12–14)

Jesus healed every person He came into contact with. Lepers were made clean, the lame could walk, the blind could see, and crippled limbs were made whole. Prostitutes became shameless, tax collectors formed soft hearts, and the dead were raised. Jesus walked in the full power of the Spirit and invites us to live in the same way. Through the Holy Spirit, we are able to see these same great works done.

And even more than this, Jesus declares that we will do even greater works.

The coming of the Messiah had been highly anticipated by the Jews for many years. The Jews longed to see the overthrow of the Roman government, and when news that the Messiah had come, they were prepared for a war.

But Jesus came humbly with teachings that turned everything upside down. He restored us to the Kingdom of Heaven and showed us what Love lived out looks like. Jesus's ministry didn't look like the world domination that the Jews expected, but what He brought was much greater.

During the time of the early church, Christians were killed relentlessly. Church history is full of martyrs that died horrible deaths for the name of Jesus. But their sacrifice spread the Gospel message faster than ever before. Often, it takes people dying for Jesus for the Good News to spread and grip hearts.

But what if no one had to die for people to know the Father's love? What if it didn't take a single martyr for people to be shook to their core with the revelation of who our Jesus is? Wouldn't it be a greater work if today, right now, an army of people stood up and took their place as sons and daughters? Isn't it a greater work that all lies and strongholds against us have been flipped over? What if we knew how completely dead to our sin we are and we walked in the fullness of the Kingdom set before us?

We live in the greater works when we allow the Kingdom to come near. We live in the greater works when we completely sell out to Jesus and run to Him with our whole hearts, letting nothing else touch us. We live in the greater works as we complete the task set before us. We live in the greater works when we usher in the Kingdom of Heaven and make room for it to completely take over this world.

We live in a blessed generation. People are done with sitting on the sidelines and standing by. The days of sitting passively in pews on Sunday are over and there is an army building of the King's children ready to walk in power. People are ready to sell-out, to give up the things of this world, and to run with everything they've got towards the One who is worthy.

Jesus is coming back, and He will be looking for the faithful on the earth. The rapture is not a rescue mission; it is a pickup for a wedding date.[1] We are participating in the rescue right now, and when you step back to look at it, we are approaching the completion of our task.

When the Great Commission was first given, there were a lot of obstacles in the way of every people group hearing the Good News. There was an undefined end of the earth, there weren't ways to travel to the unreached people, we didn't even know all the languages, there was not a large enough workforce to complete such a daunting task, and there were and still are very strict government regulations against a large number of people talking about Jesus.

Two thousand years later, there is a different report. For the first time, we are about to have knowledge of every single people group on earth. For the first time, we have global transportation that can get us across the world in a matter of hours, and we have local transportation that can get us to remote areas that aren't able to be hiked. The Bible has been translated into almost every language, and it is guessed that this project can be completed by the year 2025.[2] Our workforce has grown and is continuing to grow in numbers large enough to mobilize the entire planet, and there are organizations that know of Christians in every single country. And in areas where people aren't allowed to talk about Jesus, there have been thousands of stories and encounters of people having dreams about the Lord Jesus Christ, and because of the internet, they are able to learn who this Man is and what He has done for them.

It is not for us to know the exact moment when Christ will return, but we know that it is happening, for we are in the end-times.[3] The Pharisees were criticized for not sensing the movement of God through Jesus Christ.[4] We don't look at what the world says about the time we live in; we look to Jesus, and He shows us what is really happening. We are living in an extremely spiritually charged time. War is raging, and we have an urgency in the Spirit to press on toward our final goal.

Awaken to what God is doing in our world, for He is moving. We are living in the greater works, and most people don't even realize. The Kingdom of Heaven is on earth right now. We have a task to introduce all people to Love, Grace, and Truth. And it is happening. Wake up and join the fight. We live in a generation that can see the end in sight for the task that we have had since the beginning.

> *Jesus, thank You for Your glory. Open our eyes to the greater works and set our minds fully on the task You have given us. May we see it to completion. We boldly ask in Your name that You break every stronghold that keeps people from knowing You. Give us the courage and strength to work for the Kingdom everyday, bringing Heaven to earth by enjoying Your grace and extending Your glory. Thank You for the work of those who came before us. May we continue marching forward and bringing hearts home to You.*

Chapter 22

OUR GOLIATH

I don't like talking about satan because he's a punk and not worth my words, but I think there needs to be a few things made clear.

First of all, our sovereign God is the only being that has intrinsic power and authority. Intrinsic means originating from or belonging naturally to. God is the source of all power and authority, and He gave all of this to Jesus, who then gave it to us. The power and authority we have does not come from ourselves; we have it because God has given it to us.

Just so, the enemy has none of his own power or authority. He gets his power from us when we believe his lies. With a single word, our God can destroy him, but our good Father waits so that we have more time to bring more people home to the One who is above all things.

Also, remember that the devil is not a god—he is a fallen angel. Do not put satan and the Lord onto the same playing field, for they are not equals. Our God is far greater than lucifer ever was or ever will be. Lucifer was an angel who became obsessed with his own glory and thought himself greater than God, and so he was cast out of heaven. Pride makes satan think that he is greater than God, but of course, the king of lies believes lies. This is not some superhero movie where both sides have equal power and equal chance at winning. This is an unfair and weighted fight where there can only be one outcome. There is only one God.

And to be clear, the enemy knows what is written in the Bible. We know this because he quotes scripture to Jesus during the temptation in the wilderness.[1] If the enemy knows the Old Testament, then he knows the New Testament, and he knows the task we have been given. And if he knows the task, then he can see that we are close to completing it.

This makes him a cornered, cowering animal as his time is coming to an end. But remember that cornered animals fight more fiercely than ever before. The enemy is going to ruthlessly fight dirty as he holds onto his fleeing reign.

> For we do not wrestle against flesh and blood, but against the rulers, against the authorities, against the cosmic powers over this present darkness, against the spiritual forces of evil in the heavenly places. (Ephesians 6:12)

This war is not against people. Spiritual warfare is active and dangerous, and we need to be aware of the kind of fighting we are in. Sometimes, we don't attribute things to the works of the enemy because we don't see it in the obvious ways. There are the obvious evils of the devil—witchcraft, demon possession, war, genocide, and poverty. But there are deeper evils at work that we so often blow off as minor. Lies, fears, pornography, anxiety, depression, addictions, and distractions are all powerful weapons that are constantly used against us. And most painful of them all, an evil trick the enemy has used from the very beginning, is keeping us from knowing our true identity in Christ.

The enemy fights dirty, targeting our weaknesses and relentlessly hitting what hurts us most. This fight is against the strongholds, the lies, the fears, and the distractions that keep us from our God. We never fight people; we fight what tells people that they don't belong to God and His Kingdom.

Despite this punk that is trying to derail us, we already know that we have the ultimate victory. When David fought Goliath, he sized up his enemy; but then, he turned to the Father. And when David went into battle, he took with him a rock and a slingshot. When we know who our God is, we can walk with confidence knowing that we will win. The only weapon we need is the power of the Word that is alive and active and sharper than any sword.[2] The Word goes before us and nothing can stand in the way of Truth. The Word prepares a banquet before us in the presence of our enemies.

Remember who your God is. Rest at His table; sit in His peace. You are safe in His salvation and in the knowledge of His glory. All you need is a rock and a slingshot. Remember God and fight with Him for your brothers and sisters who don't yet know Him. Fight for your family who has been taken hostage by a world that is broken and lying to them.

Fight focused with Jesus as the One set before you. Remember His goodness and His faithfulness and hold your head high as you walk as His warrior. Remember the cross and the glory of our Lord. Jesus is worth your life, and nothing can touch you when He is with you.

Jesus, thank You for winning this war for us already. Thank You Lord, that You are the only God. There is no one beside You—no one like You. Remind us that we only need a rock to win because You have done it. Give us focus so that we never get tired, so we can keep running with You. May we never make this fight against flesh. Teach us to see the works of the enemy for what they are. And may we be a people who always have Your glory in mind, for You are greater, stronger, and mightier and worthy to be praised.

Chapter 23

IF YOU ARE

> Then Jesus was led up by the Spirit into the wilderness to be tempted by the devil. And after fasting forty days and forty nights, he was hungry. And the tempter came and said to him, "If you are the Son of God. . . ." (Matthew 4:1–3)

And here we see the great lie that the enemy uses time and time again. It's his biggest card—his knockout punch. And we know he is going to use it against us because he used it against the Savior five seconds into trying to tempt Jesus into sinning.

On the surface this jab plays at pride, verbally doubting truth, which could then lead someone to work to prove who they really are. But there's a deeper and poisonous root that can take hold with the statement "if you are."

If we always wonder "if," we question who we are and who God is. This statement is used to get us to react with our pride, and if that doesn't work, it dives into undermining what we really think about ourselves. And if we are always wondering if we really are who God says we are and if God is who He says He is, then we are already taken out of the fight against the enemy. If the liar can keep us wondering, he removes us from the battlefield. Distracted and unaware soldiers are useless and can even be dangerous to their own army.

But there's a combative statement to any "if you are" question. And it starts with God—"Since He is." This is the beginning of everything we should believe about ourselves and others.

Since He is King, we are royalty. Since He has adopted us, we are no longer orphans. Since He is our Father, we are His children. Since He is the Good Shepherd, we are His sheep. Since He is good, we are taken care of. Since He is Immanuel, we have God with us.

Remember your adoption and remember who you are. But most importantly, know that everything you are is because of who He is. He comes first, so stop questioning who you are and know who He is. He did not make a mistake with you; He designed and created you, as well as prepared and planned a place for you.

Don't believe lies and don't partner with fear. Never wonder "if you are" because you know that He is. He has bought you with a price, for you belong to Christ. You are loved, cherished, and longed for in deeper ways than you can imagine. Nothing can change who God is; therefore, nothing can change who you are. Focus on Jesus, for when we fix our eyes on Him, everything else falls into place.

Learn His voice and know His touch. For what we can accomplish on this earth is a matter of the heart.

> Not everyone who says to me, "Lord, Lord," will enter the kingdom of heaven, but the one who does the will of my Father who is in heaven. On that day many will say to me, "Lord, Lord, did we not prophesy in your name, and cast out demons in your name, and do many mighty works in your name?' and then will I declare to them, 'I never knew you; depart from me, you workers of lawlessness." (Matthew 7:21–23)

We can do great things and still miss the point. For even if we do great things, what do we really have if we don't walk with Jesus? Without Him, everything is worthless. Jesus doesn't want our works—He wants our hearts.

Don't just know about God—know God. We have been invited to actively participate in the most intimate relationship. We have been invited to sit at the King's table, and our Father has big plans for us. He boldly declares nothing but good things for us.

> "For I know the plans I have for you," declares the Lord, "plans to prosper you and not to harm you, plans to give you a hope and a future." (Jeremiah 29:11; NIV)

So many of us like to stop right there. But the Lord doesn't stop talking there; we just tend to stop listening. He continues:

> Then you will call upon me and come and pray to me, and I will hear you. You will seek me and find me, when you seek me with all your heart. I will be found by you, declares the Lord, and I will restore your fortunes and gather you from all the nations and all the places where I have driven you, declares the Lord, and I will bring you back to the place from which I sent you into exile. (Jeremiah 29:12–14)

We like to stop after verse 11 because we are focused on ourselves. This one verse is empowering and encouraging, but there's more that comes after it. There's a reason that we are blessed.

Everything we do and receive should point us back to Him. This intimate relationship we are led into isn't a new design. The place that we were exiled from, the place we are being brought back to, is Eden. We are able to dwell, live, and smile with the One who created it all.

Position yourself to do great things by wrapping your heart around His. Value your relationship with the Father more than any blessing, plan, or favor that you receive. Keep your focus on Him, never looking away from the King.

There is no question of who you are because He is good. Stop trying to fight for something that you already have received. Rest in who He says you are and walk with Him in the abundant life that He has given you. The question of "if you are" is irrelevant because He is.

Papa, thank You for giving us Your Son. Thank You for clearly revealing Your heart to us. Remove anything in us that keeps us from longing to know You more. May we stop being a people who know about You and become people who walk intently with You in the garden. May we be a people who never questions "if we are" again. Align our hearts with Yours so that we can love You better and do great things with You. Thank You for already taking care of everything for us so that we can be completely devoted and focused on You. Thank You for Your steadfast love and abundant blessings. Give us today a new revelation of who You are, so that we can love You with our whole heart.

Chapter 24

CALLINGS

The law is satisfied and we are free to live in all the abundant blessings that Christ has waiting for us. Once we had a law that dictated how we could be right with God, but now we have the life of Christ as our example for how we are to live, along with the disciples and apostles who have gone before us that show what life can look like in the Kingdom.

So we have a new understanding of the task before us, but the question remains of how we are going to do it. And with this question in mind, sometimes we start to long for a calling. We want a specific and detailed plan that will map out direction for our entire life.

People want a road map, but more often the directions we receive look more like a compass. Maps focus on directions rather than direction, while compasses focus on purpose rather than plans. Our God knows both, but when He instructs us He tends to give compass movements rather than map coordinates.

For example, Abraham is told he will be the father of many nations in Genesis 17. This goal and purpose for his life is extraordinary and exciting, but the instructions he receives to do such a thing are lacking. He is simply told to "Go to the land I will show you." These instructions are brief and aren't even given until Genesis 21, a good amount of time after the first call.

Sometimes we see extremely specific instructions given, like in Genesis 6 when Noah is directed to build the ark and is told the exact measurements, layout, and materials to use. More often however our directions come like Abraham's did, and there is a reason for this.

Simple and vague instructions help to build our trust and faith in God and His perfect timing. They also teach reliance on the Father so that we learn to be looking to Him for the next steps. But there's something even more beautiful and wonderful that happens when we aren't given step by step life instructions. And that is, we learn to live with God rather than for God.

What God is saying when He doesn't tell us specifically what to do is, "Just come be with Me", because we are called to Someone before we are called to something.[1] The Father invites us to live with Him, to learn from Him, and be loved by Him. Even in Noah's case, it says in verse 9 that even before Noah received the instructions for the ark, that Noah was a righteous man who "walked with God".

The Father wants to do life with you, whatever you decide to do. He trusts you to make decisions in your life because He pursues your heart. He doesn't want you to try to fit Him into your life and plan. Align your heart with His and your mindset with His mission plan, and see what can happen.

God is everywhere and wants to move everywhere. The places our hearts are drawn to the most are more than likely the places that He is asking us specifically to go. He wants passionate people doing what they love. There are so many people, and places, and things in this world and not one person, or one personality type, or one occupation can reach every person. You don't have to be in full time ministry to spread the Kingdom. In fact, we need Christians invading every area of this earth.

With a heart after the Lord, you will not step out of His desires. When you are only looking to the King, you will not make a wrong life decision. Your faith is in Jesus, not yourself. Walk with Him, delight in Him as He delights in you. Our Father wants to give us good things, things that are tailored to our hearts. He will bless the decisions we make as we seek His Kingdom first.

If you need something more than this, remember that Jesus always went to the lost, the broken, and the hurting. Jesus relentlessly pursued the outcasts, and we should be too.

You are called to be a worshipper. Praise Him always with a pure heart and you will make mountains move. Live a life that abounds in thanksgiving. Pull Heaven down with your worship. Enjoy His grace.

You are called to make disciples. People are hungry for Jesus, be a witness in word and in deed. Ask for the Father's heart for His people and extravagantly love every person you encounter. You are also called to go. Go to your work, the grocery store, the local church, other states, other countries, other continents. Everywhere you go, walk with Jesus, intentionally looking for ways to love people. Extend His glory, bring people home.

When I was younger, I wanted to work with animals. I know, shocking that a little girl had dreams of being a veterinarian. As I got a little older I started working with horses and decided I could make a nice living for myself being a horse doctor, and that became the plan.

I remember there was one day when I was in high school that my Grandpa said to me, "You know Mel, I just don't understand why someone would want to help animals when there are so many people who need help." And I realized he was right. I looked for a way to combine helping people and working with horses, and started to set my heart on equine therapy, which is using horses to help people with different needs.

As I headed off to college I pursued a degree in Animal Science. My plan was for my undergrad to be in horses and then I would pair it with a Masters in counseling of some kind to then have a career of using horses to help people. I've always been a planner and I loved being able to tell people with confidence what my future career would be. However, my perfectly mapped out plan soon got distorted.

During my fourth semester of college I started hearing a lot of sermons on course corrections. I started to wonder if the plan for me to work with horses was my plan or the Lord's. I felt like He was asking me if I would give up horses for Him, and so I jumped away from the barn as quickly as I could. I realized I had developed a heart for helping people, but I was hiding in the barn. I had figured that people wouldn't want my help directly, so I would draw them in with horses first.

I started my fifth and final semester of college confused and a little panicked. I would be graduating in a matter of months and I had no idea what was going to happen after. I didn't even know what city I was going to be living in until the month of graduation. It was frustrating to go from having all the plans to having none, but I learned a lot in the process.

I learned how to let go. I learned more about freedom. I learned what not planning looks like and ended up loving it. I learned how to be okay answering almost every question with "I don't know." I learned how to stop striving and I learned more about living with Jesus instead of for Him. I learned how to be content within today. And I learned that if you pursue Jesus, you will see the ways that He is already pursuing you.

I may still work with horses; I love training troublesome ponies and teaching others how to ride. I may still get a Masters in some undecided area of study. Or I could find some other crazy career to fall in love with. I have no clue what I will do or what my life will look like.

By the world's standards, it doesn't look like I'm doing too well. I'm not using my degree or pursing any sort of career, I moved back in with my parents for who knows how long, and I only have 325 followers on Instagram. But I have learned to use a different measurement when I look at my success.

Kingdom success is daily loving Jesus with a whole heart, walking in step with Him, and helping others do the same. Whatever that ends up looking like, life is fun and enjoyable with compass purpose rather than mapped directions. There is freedom and excitement as I live with Him and experience His goodness, without pressure to perform or to be something that I'm not. I let my heart draw me and I listen to the gentle nudges of the Shepherd as I figure out what it means to be human.

Sometimes it's completely frustrating not knowing what I want to do, and sometimes it's great. The only plan I have is to love Jesus every day and to see where it takes me. So far, it has led me to numerous countries and given me an itch to see more. It has led me to love on countless people and to have strong and meaningful friendships. And it has even led me to writing a book that I hope will help others be able to love the Father more deeply as well.

I still have questions and confusion regarding the exact direction that my life will take, and you may too. But all I can say is to simply walk with Him. Position your heart before Him and He will bless you in this life. There is no more striving, no pressure to perform. The Lord's timing is perfect and He will bring us to where we need to be when we need to be there. Rest, relax, and let Him draw near to your heart. Step by step, day by day, love Him with all your heart, and you will experience the abundant life Christ bought for you.

> *Jesus thank You for living a life that is an example to us. May we learn how to live daily as worshippers. Teach us to boldly walk in Your power, not being afraid of the future. Give us Your heart so that we may align our desires with Yours. Help us to keep You at the center of our entire lives. Thank You for walking so closely with us and may we start to recognize the things You do for us every day. Set our hearts on fire for You so that we may show this world who You really are.*

Chapter 25

KINGDOM CULTURE

You've more than likely heard the phrase "when in Rome" at least once in your life. The phrase in its entirety is actually "when in Rome, do as the Romans do." This phrase came from the days of the Roman Empire. As the Romans conquered, the areas they took over were molded to look like the home city of Rome. But this didn't happen overnight.

As the Romans began to take land, they would often go back to territories they had already conquered and find that the city had reversed back to its own rule, disregarding Roman law. In order to stop this, the Romans began to send their teachers, philosophers, city planners, governors, and other trained positions with the Roman soldiers. After conquering a city, some of the soldiers and the Roman professionals would stay in the city to change the culture. The Romans learned early on that if you do not change the culture, there will be no lasting change. Through this method of conquering, the Roman Empire was vast and strong and surely the sun never set on Rome.

The process of changing culture is not easy, but it is necessary if the Kingdom of Heaven is going to invade the kingdom of earth. Too many people today have accepted a church culture that does not fit Kingdom culture. Discover Kingdom culture so that you will never settle for less.

The Kingdom is pure joy! When I first started walking in the Kingdom, I had just finished the worst semester of my life. I was depressed and devastated and resigned to stay in that state indefinitely. But Jesus came in and reminded me of joy—His joy. I marched forward into the Kingdom with this joy and have held onto it ever since. Joy is a key component of Kingdom culture, and we rejoice because we do not live in a boring and dull kingdom—but one of life, laughter, and pure joy!

> Rejoice in the Lord always; again I will say, rejoice. (Philippians 4:4)

Kingdom culture is one of prayer and worship. Everywhere we go, we should bring the Kingdom through our bold prayers and joyful praise to our God. We need to set a precedent that we will be a people who value the presence of our Lord, cultivating His Spirit within us and praying in His name at all times. Prayer is one of the best forms of worship, and praise for the Lord should always be on the tip of our tongues. And the Kingdom is pure joy! We do not serve a dull and boring god, for our Savior is full of life and color and fun.

A prayerful culture is more powerful than we realize. Our Father is faithful to our prayers, and therefore, we can pray with boldness and confidence. Our words have power because we bring life into this world by the words we speak.

Praying outwardly is a part of Kingdom culture. Stop speaking the problems you see around you and start praying into the solution. When we start to pray fervently for the people around us, we can begin to see the Kingdom take over like never before. Pray for other people because you know that the Lord has and will continue to take care of you. Selfish prayers often consume people, and we undermine the power we have within us when we don't use our prayers to bring favor and blessings to those around us.

Offer everything to God and listen to what He has to give back to you. Our prayers are not one sided, for He longs to respond to the things we tell Him. Spend time sitting in prayer, listening to what He may have to say to you. And always, without exception, offer praise to the King. He is enthroned on our praises, and we usher in the Kingdom by praising Him daily.

Kingdom culture lives in the current moment, for the Kingdom of Heaven is today. Live within the means of today.

> Therefore do not be anxious, saying, "What shall we eat?" or "What shall we drink?" or "What shall we wear?" For the Gentiles seek after all these things, and your heavenly Father knows that you need them all. But seek first the kingdom of God and his righteousness, and all these things will be added to you. Therefore do not be anxious about tomorrow, for tomorrow will be anxious for itself. Sufficient for the day is its own trouble. (Matthew 6:31–34)

We are given daily bread, which means we are given everything we need to live today to the fullest. Thinking too much about tomorrow takes away from enjoying the blessings of today. Our daily bread is Jesus, and He longs to meet with us today, in every moment. The Kingdom is advanced as we learn to live fully within today.

Living in today gives us vision for tomorrow. If our life is a puzzle, our Father wants to start giving us the pieces to begin working them into a masterpiece. Sometimes, we take the single piece He is handing us and we make it the entire picture, or we start to think of what the next piece might be. Take the pieces He is giving you and place them where they need to go. He knows what the picture is; we don't have to. Diligently seek the Kingdom today, and let Him work out the puzzle for you. Doing this will result in a beautiful picture that you would not be able to muster on your own.

Jesus wants to bless us within today, and Kingdom culture is advanced as we take each day as it comes, living each moment to the fullest. Seek first His Kingdom, and let Him sort everything else out for you. Kingdom culture lives in today.

Be a good son and a good brother. Love God and love those around you. The Kingdom is family-oriented, so be disciplined and practiced in being a good family member. We are all invited into the most powerful family around, and it's time we take this seriously. Ask God for His heart so that you can genuinely love the people around you.

The law of the Kingdom is love. Love is Kingdom culture. Make the decision to love. Don't operate out of feelings, for feelings are good to supplement our lives but they should not lead us or be deciding factors. Love is a choice, not a feeling. Love every and all without exception or expectation. Learn how to love well. Learn how to love from Love Himself. Fight for Love because Love has already won for you.

Love is easy for we have seen it lived out in Jesus Christ. Mimic Him who has known you since the beginning. Love is divinely woven into your creation, so bring the Kingdom to earth by delving into Love. Let Rabbi Jesus teach you how to love, and His Kingdom will spread like wildfire. For we don't bring people into the Kingdom through arguments, but by loving and encouraging them to see the Father for who He really is.

> Now when Jesus came into the district of Caesarea Philippi, he asked his disciples, "Who do people say the Son of Man is?" And they said, "Some say John the Baptist, others say Elijah, and others Jeremiah or one of the prophets." He said to them, "But who do you say that I am?" Simon Peter replied, "You are the Christ, the Son of the living God." And Jesus answered him, "Blessed are you, Simon Bar-Jonah! For flesh and blood has not revealed this to you, but my Father who is in heaven. And I tell you, you are Peter, and on this rock I will build my church, and the gates of hell shall not prevail against it. I will give you the keys of the kingdom of heaven, and whatever you bind on earth shall be bound in heaven, and whatever you loose on earth shall be loosed in heaven." (Matthew 16:13–19)

Jesus gives us the keys to the Kingdom! Through His life, Jesus shows us what we are to do with these keys. We are to freely and passionately give them to everyone. Peter used the keys he was given to start the Church, and we need more key holders today to continue this work. Unlock for others the things that have been opened for you.

Our Kingdom is unshakable because of the rock it is built on, which is Jesus as the Christ—the Son of the living God. This is the key—This is the entrance into the Kingdom of Heaven. Kingdom culture is one that gives out keys to every person we encounter. Our Kingdom is not secret, and it is not exclusive.

What are you going to do with the keys that have been given to you?

> *Jesus, thank You for a Kingdom unlike any other. Thank You for orchestrating the puzzle for us, and thank You for being a good and kind teacher. Teach us to be active Kingdom members. Teach us the culture of Your Kingdom; teach us Kingdom principles that we are to live from. Teach us to live within today and give us vision for tomorrow. Teach us to love. Lord may we be the Church that You desire us to be. May we step into all that You have prepared for us, and may the Kingdom of Heaven invade the earth that we live in.*

Chapter 26

BATTLE CRY

It's time for you to make the decision to live in the Kingdom of Heaven. Daily decide to be a worshipper who will praise His name and work to spread His glory.

We need you, just as you are. You play a greater part than you ever imagined. There are people all around you who need to hear the Good News, and you need to tell them.

We need men to stand up and take their place as spiritual leaders. We need women to step into the purity of a worshipper to show the world how to praise the Father. We need moms and dads to become Spirit-led and show their family how to walk in the way of Truth. We need sons and daughters to know their Father. We need Kingdom brothers and sisters to look after their siblings struggling around them. We need doctors and waiters and pastors and students and missionaries and builders and drivers and salesmen and CEOs and janitors and people of every single occupation to know that they are dearly loved children and that they are capable of bringing the Kingdom where they are today.

We need you to step up and take your rightful place in the Kingdom. Today, choose to fight for the One who has already won. You are chosen by God to bring Heaven to earth. Enjoy His grace; extend His glory.

Every time I think about the Kingdom of Heaven, a battle cry screams within me. I can hear William Wallace's triumphant scream of "Freedom!" at the end of *Braveheart*. The Spirit within me yearns for the world to know the Father that I know and love.

The Kingdom is a part of me as much as I am a part of it. I long for the Spirit to be able to move within me and through me so that the Lamb may have His reward.

You are the reward for the suffering of the Lamb. The Kingdom is yours, so rise up and take your rightful place as a child of the One true King.

We need you to fight for freedom. Fight to bring Heaven to earth today. Take up your sword, which is the Word of Truth, and destroy every wall and barrier that keeps you and anyone else from knowing who the Lord is. Flip tables. Allow the power of the Spirit to flow out of you and rejoice as Jesus brings all people to Himself.

Fight focused on Jesus and watch as the Kingdom of Heaven invades the fallen world. May the Lamb that was slain receive the reward for His suffering.

> *Jesus, Your Kingdom come, Your will be done on earth as it is in Heaven. Teach us to be Kingdom-minded and instill in us a never-dying passion of seeing Your will be done. Set a fire in our souls that leads us to usher in the Kingdom of Heaven.*

Only the Beginning

Chapter 27

MOVEMENT

I have worked with horses for many years and one of the things I enjoy the most is training them, especially groundwork. Horses respond to pressure and learn through the release of pressure. This means that we apply pressure and only release when the horse responds in the way we desire. Pressure can be a variety of things—a sound, moving your arm, waving a whip, a touch, or anything that makes the horse uncomfortable enough to move. We release the pressure when the horse moves in the way we are wanting, and soon, the horse knows what we are asking him to do.

Horses react differently to pressure, and you have to learn what is going to work for the horse you are currently training. Some horses need very little incentive to move, making them not only reactive but also often quick learners.

The worst horses to train are those that need a lot of pressure to get them to move. These are the stubborn horses that will wear you out fast, as you have to expend lots of energy to get any sort of movement out of them.

Movement is essential in horse training, as well as our lives in the Kingdom. God can do a lot with a person who is willing to try things and step out into the unknown. Be ready and willing to move at even the slightest nudge from the King. Be obedient and willing.

You will be amazed at what God can do through you if you just become willing to move.

> When they heard this, they were enraged and wanted to kill them. But a Pharisee in the council named Gamaliel, a teacher of the law held in honor by all the people, stood up and gave orders to put the men outside for a little while. And he said to them, "Men of Israel, take care what you are about to do with these men. For before these days Theudas rose up, claiming to be somebody, and a number of men, about four hundred, joined him. He was killed, and all who followed him were dispersed and came to noting. After him Judas the Galilean rose up in the days of the census and drew away some of the people after him. He too perished, and all who followed him were scattered. So in the present case I tell you, keep away from these men and let them alone, for if this plan or this undertaking is of man, it will fail; but if it is of God, you will not be able to overthrow them. You might even be found opposing God!" (Acts 5:33–39)

Move, for if what you are doing is of God, you will not fail! For if God is for us, who can be against us?[1]

Move because you are a chosen agent of change. You are needed to spread God's glory throughout the earth. God is capable of working without us, but He has chosen us to co-labor with Him.

> The earth was without form and void, and darkness was over the face of the deep. And the Spirit of God was hovering over the face of the waters. (Genesis 1:2)

The Spirit hovered over the waters, waiting—waiting in anticipation, waiting with the full power of the Creator. And as soon as God spoke, the Spirit moved. The Spirit waits for the Word to be spoken before moving in power.

This Spirit is now within us, waiting for us to speak. When we speak the Word into this world, the Spirit moves in power. We are able to operate within the full power of the Spirit; but we need to move, we need to speak, so that this power can manifest. Move so that the Spirit of God that is within you can move. Attempt great things for God and you can expect great things from God.[2]

The message is simple. The Gospel is not complicated. Jesus's messages are simple, but that doesn't mean it is easy. Believe what He says, and follow Him. Surrender isn't about giving everything up; it's about finding something worth giving everything for. And Jesus is worth it, forever and always. Value His presence, cultivate the Kingdom, and be a worshiper.

We are designed for the adventure of a lifetime. You are daily given the opportunity to participate in something greater than yourself, and the possibilities are endless. Move, do something, make room for more. Find movement in your life so that the Spirit can flow out of you. To start this great adventure, you must be brave enough to take a step forward. Jesus is ready, are you?

> *Jesus, help us move. Help us speak life into this world. May Your Word go before us. Thank You for filling us with Your power. Thank You that it is truly a simple gospel. Give us the courage, strength, and endurance to complete the task that is set before us. May we forever be a people who value Your presence and Your Kingdom. May we be a people that You desire Father. Thank You for loving us, always.*

Chapter 28

FURTHER

Awaken to the great works being done. Renew your mind and see what is in store for you. Rejoice as you witness dead bones coming to life!

To see the Kingdom come has been my heart cry and constant prayer every day since I knew the love of my Savior. And every day I long to experience His love deeper and more fully.

These things I have written out I have learned through walking in the Kingdom, and I am excited to share them with anyone who will listen. But please don't just take my word on anything. Seek these things for yourself. Dig deeper into the Word; discover what He is trying to tell you about Himself. Taste and see! Knock and be answered! Come to Him and you will not be disappointed.

There is more in store for you than just an ordinary life. The supernatural works of the Spirit are within your reach, but more than that, there is deeper love and acceptance for you than you ever imagined possible. Love awaits you.

Put on the Kingdom and be pleasantly surprised at how right and comfortable it feels. Come home to the place you were made for."Further in and higher up!"[1] Dive deeper into what is awaiting you in Heaven. Come home today and rejoice! Let the words of C. S. Lewis resonate within you as you begin to discover the Kingdom of Heaven today, on earth.

"I have come home at last! This is my real country! I belong here. This is the land I have been looking for all my life, though I never knew it till now. The reason why we loved the old Narnia is that it sometimes looked a little like this. . . Come further up, come further in!"[2]

Learning truth doesn't do much for you, but applying truth has the power to transform lives. Choose to believe in yourself today by believing God and who He says you are. Choose to love everyone and praying boldly for others. Choose to value the gift of community by being a good brother. Choose to walk with Jesus and to seek His Kingdom first.

Move deeper and deeper into His Kingdom and be transformed from glory to glory![3] And rejoice! For we do not serve a god who is distant and uninterested, but we serve the One who is near and sovereign and who loves us more deeply than we may ever know.

> *Abba, thank You for longing to speak with Your people. Thank You for speaking to us and drawing near. Thank You for the many blessings you pour out relentlessly on us. Thank You for making us right with You and for always keeping us in Your gaze. Thank You for Truth, Grace, and Love. Thank You for setting us up for success and for filling us with Your Spirit. We praise You because You are good. You are kind and wonderful and faithful and worthy of all praise. You are mighty and beautiful and full of splendor. You are Love. You are our Savior, our Healer, our Helper, and our Creator. Lord You are everything to us; may we give everything to You.*
>
> *Father, Your Kingdom come, on earth as it is in heaven.*

NOTES

All Bible passages taken from the English Standard Version unless otherwise specified.

Chapter 1: Are You Ready?

    1.   J. K. Rowing, "Harry Potter and the Sorcerer's Stone" (New York: Scholastic Press, 1998), 50.

Chapter 2: His Love

    1.   Judah Smith: Love, Part 1 "The One You Love" with Judah Smith, Lifechurch.tv, sermon paraphrased by M. R. Renkema.
    2.   John 11:1-44
    3.   John 11:33-35
    4.   Matthew 26:75
    5.   John 21:15–19

Chapter 3: Rags to Riches

    1.   Genesis 17:1–5
    2.   Ibid., 17:15
    3.   Kris Vallotton and Bill Johnson, "The Supernatural Ways of Royalty," paraphrased by M. R. Renkema (Pennsylvania: Destiny Images Publishers, 2006), 218–219.
    4.   Genesis 14:12
    5.   Ibid., 13:1–13

6. Ibid., 19:26
7. Ibid., 19:12–13
8. Ibid., 19:17
9. Ibid., 18:11–12
10. Matthew 5:13
11. Todd White, quote paraphrased by M. R. Renkema.
12. Nina Kazarian: The Hidden Treasure, ninamarianna.com, blog paraphrased by M. R. Renkema.
13. Todd White, quote paraphrased by M. R. Renkema.

Chapter 4: Orphans No More

1. Sandra L. Richter, summary, "The Epic of Eden" (Illinois: InterVarsity Press, 2008), 25–33.
2. Ephesians 2:1

Chapter 5: Jars of Clay

1. John 16:33

Chapter 6: Roots and Fruits

1. Galatians 5:22–23

Chapter 7: The Still Small Voice

1. Bethel Sozo Training: Colored Lenses/The Wall, paraphrased by M. R. Renkema
2. Ibid.
3. Ibid., Presenting Jesus, paraphrased by M. R. Renkema

Chapter 10: The Name of God

1. Brennan Manning, "The Relentless Tenderness of Jesus," paraphrased by M. R. Renkema (Michigan: Revell, 2004), 17.

2. Bill Johnson, "God is Good," paraphrased by M. R. Renkema (Pennsylvania: Destiny Image Publishers, 2016), 118.
3. Bethel Sozo Training: The Father Ladder, summary
4. Author's visual representation of the Father Ladder from Bethel Sozo Training: The Father Ladder

Chapter 11: Shameless

1. Concept from Chris Gore. (2014) Healing School, New Covenant Fellowship, Stillwater, Oklahoma, February 3–5, 2017.
2. Nina Kazarian: The Walking Scandal: Shame & Freedom, ninamarianna.com, blog summary

Chapter 12: But Jesus

1. Chris Gore, summary (2014) Healing School, New Covenant Fellowship, Stillwater, Oklahoma, February 3–5, 2017.
2. Ibid., paraphrased by M. R. Renkema
3. Ibid.

Chapter 13: Reset

1. Lisa Bevere, "Without Rival," paraphrased by M. R. Renkema (Michigan: Revell, 2016), 19.
2. Ibid., 18.
3. Matthew 5:44
4. Luke 10:25–37
5. John 13:34
6. Ephesians 6:12
7. Matthew 25:40

Chapter 14: Heartbeat

1. Hawthorne, Steven. 'The Great Commission and The Great Commandment'. *Perspectives on The World Christian Movement*. Eds. Ralph D. Winter and Steven C. Hawthorne. Pasadena: William Carey Library, 2009. 128–129. Print, summary.
2. Jon Odom: Love Your Neighbor, Asbury United Methodist Church, Tulsa, Oklahoma, January 22, 2017, sermon paraphrased by M. R. Renkema.
3. Pastor Tom Harrison, Senior Pastor at Asbury United Methodist Church in Tulsa, Oklahoma, quote paraphrased by M. R. Renkema.

Chapter 15: Uncommon

1. Acts 10:22
2. Acts 10:30–48

Chapter 17: Sheepfold

1. 2 Corinthians 3:18
2. Rick Davis, Perspectives Speaker: Week 1, quote paraphrased by M. R. Renkema.

Chapter 18: Eden

1. Genesis 2:8
2. Ibid. 2:16
3. Ibid. 1:28

Chapter 19: Israel

1. List of scriptures shortened from Perspectives Class: Week 1
2. Rick Davis, Perspectives Speaker: Week 1, quote paraphrased by M. R. Renkema.

Chapter 20: Flipping Tables

1. Nathan Allen, Perspectives Speaker: Week 6
2. Acts 1:3
3. John 2:6–9

Chapter 21: Status Report

1. Todd White, quote paraphrased by M. R. Renkema.
2. Projection from Wycliffe Bible Translators, Dennis Cochrane, Perspectives Speaker: Week 3
3. 1 Peter 4:7
4. John 8:48–59

Chapter 22: Our Goliath

1. Matthew 4:1–11
2. Hebrews 4:12

Chapter 24: Callings

1. R. Paul Stevens, "Work Matters," paraphrased by M. R. Renkema (Michigan: Wm. B. Eerdman's Publishing Co., 2012), 33.

Chapter 27: Movement

1. Romans 8:31
2. William Carey, quote paraphrased by M. R. Renkema.

Chapter 28: Further

1. C. S. Lewis, "The Chronicles of Narnia: The Last Battle" (New York: Scholastic Inc., 1984), 176.
2. Ibid., 196.
3. 2 Corinthians 3:18

ABOUT THE AUTHOR

Melissa grew up in a Christian family and has been faithfully walking in step with Jesus since January 2015. Melissa has a heart for the Church and longs to see it become the beloved Bride of Christ. She is passionate about inner healing and loves to work with youth and college students, helping them learn how to hear God's voice and helping them to discover who they were created to be. Melissa's goal is to equip the saints and to teach them to walk in power. She emphasizes the importance of prayer and loves teaching God's word. She longs for the nations and eagerly prays for world revival.

Melissa loves traveling, especially for missions. She leads a small group of high school students and enjoys accompanying them on mission trips, retreats, and camps because in these times, Heaven comes to earth in big and powerful ways. She has a servant's heart and loves working for her city, Tulsa, Oklahoma. She enjoys reading and training horses.

Melissa passionately and diligently follows the Lord's direction in her life. She wrote this book in six weeks as she obediently formed words for the things that Jesus was whispering to her. The urgency she feels is just a part of her desire to see people know the Creator—Father, Savior and Helper.

Liked this book?

COMING SOON!

Engaging the Kingdom

Here's a sneak peek into the next book by this author.

Chapter 1

AWAKEN

There is an epidemic of people not living out their birth right. There are people walking around who know the name of Jesus but don't live in the Kingdom that He established for us. The Church has fallen asleep in their pew. And it's time to engage.

In John 10 Jesus beautifully describes life in His Kingdom, and in verse 9 He says, "I am the door. If anyone enters by me, he will be saved and will go in and out and find pasture." We come to the cross and we are saved, but that's just the entrance. We enter by grace, and then we live abundantly with Jesus.

Going in and out refers to life as a part of His flock. His sheep walk with Him and do life with Him, daily going in and out of their paddock. We live in step with the Shepherd, among wolves unharmed because we are covered in His blood. And not only do we go in and out, but we also find pasture. We are wrapped in His care, and we will always have what is essential.

There is a whole life to live with Christ, the abundant life that He came to give us. There are realms to explore that He has already given us the keys to. We have His Kingdom on earth today and have been given every right to walk within it.

But there's a problem, people keep stopping at the door. Standing in the doorway of salvation only gives you a small glimpse of the Kingdom of Heaven. We were made to march tall on this earth, taking back what belongs to the Father, bringing Heaven to earth.

The importance of the Kingdom is written throughout the Gospels. Jesus's main message was about ushering in the Kingdom, and He even tells us to seek the Kingdom first, above food, clothes, and security.[1] But we have fallen asleep. The Church has become numb to the Kingdom we were created for. And it's no surprise the Jesus already warned us about this.

> Then Jesus went with them to a place called Gethsemane, and he said to his disciples, "Sit here, while I go over there and pray." And taking with him Peter and the two sons of Zebedee, he began to be sorrowful and troubled. Then he said to them, "My soul is very sorrowful, even to death; remain here, and watch with me." And going a little farther he fell on his face and prayed, saying, "My Father, if it be possible, let this cup pass from me; nevertheless, not as I will, but as you will." And he came to the disciples and found them sleeping. And he said to Peter, "So, could you not watch with me one hour? Watch and pray that you may not enter into temptation. The spirit indeed is willing, but the flesh is weak." Again, for the second time, he went away and prayed, "My Father, if this cannot pass unless I drink it, your will be done." And again he came and found them sleeping, for their eyes were heavy. So, leaving them again, he went away and prayed for the third time, saying the same words again. Then he came to the disciples and said to

them, "Sleep and take your rest later on. See, the hour is at hand, and the Son of Man is betrayed into the hands of sinners. Rise, let us be going; see, my betrayer is at hand." (Matthew 26:36-46)

Jesus tells them to watch and pray, and pray specifically that they may not fall into temptation. Jesus doesn't tell them to pray for Him, because the walk of the cross starts in the garden. His emotional torment is the beginning of the greatest Spiritual battle ever fought. Jesus was ready for what He was stepping into, and He wanted to make sure His disciples would be too.

As Jesus takes the cross, the disciples' lives change forever. Their next few days are full of grief, relief, and confusion as they first see Jesus dead, and then just a few days later they hear He is alive. They begin to encounter Him, see Him, and touch Him. They break bread with Him once more as they are strengthened for their task. They wait together until the Holy Spirit falls on them, and then their mission booms.

They form the Church and they begin to make more disciples. They hand out keys to the Kingdom and start the work of bringing the Good News to every tongue, tribe, and nation. They operate within the full power of the Spirit and they never stop charging forward, taking more and more ground for the Kingdom of Heaven.

For the rest of their lives they labor full force. Most of them are severally persecuted, even dying terrible deaths for the sake of the Gospel. The Church today and any person who knows the name of Jesus is because of the single minded focus that the Apostles had in their mission.

But back in that garden, they didn't know this was coming. These men had no idea what they were about to be stepping into, and so they are told to watch and pray. Jesus wanted them to start their mission saturated in prayer.

But they fall asleep, and this is what the Church has done today. Jesus tells them to pray that they may not fall into temptation because there is the tendency to become numb to the Kingdom. The Church has always been tempted to take the easy path and to sleep as the world groans and aches. But this is not the life of Kingdom people. Kingdom people are alive, invested, and engaged. But there is temptation to sleep, and that is why Jesus tells them to pray. And He knew they needed to do so because this is not a new problem.

In Genesis 18 we see this happening. To give you some background, in Genesis 17 God established His covenant with Abraham. In verse 5, Abram gets his new name and becomes Abraham, and in verse 15 Abraham's wife goes from Sarai to Sarah. In verse 16 Abraham is told that Sarah will have a child, and in verse 17 Abraham laughs because he says that Sarah is too old to have a child. In verses 19 and 21, Isaac is foretold and God says that His covenant will continue in Isaac. This brings us to Genesis 18.

> And the Lord appeared to him by the oaks of Mamre, as he sat at the door of his tent in the heat of the day. He lifted up his eyes and looked, and behold, three men were standing in front of him. When he saw them, he ran from the tent door to meet them and bowed himself to the earth and said, "O Lord, if I have found favor in your sight, do not pass by your servant. Let a little water be brought, and wash your feet, and rest yourselves under the tree, while I bring a morsel of bread, that you may refresh yourselves, and after that you may pass on—since you have come to your servant." So they said, "Do as you have said." And Abraham went quickly into the tent to Sarah and said, "Quick! Three seahs of fine flour! Knead it, and make cakes." And Abraham ran to the herd and took a calf, tender and good, and gave it to a young man, who prepared it quickly. Then he took curds and milk and the calf that he had prepared, and set it before them. And he stood by them under the tree while they ate.
> They said to him, "Where is Sarah your wife?" And he said, "She is in the tent." The

Lord said, "I will surely return to you about this time next year, and Sarah your wife shall have a son." And Sarah was listening at the tent door behind him. Now Abraham and Sarah were old, advanced in years. The way of women had ceased to be with Sarah. So Sarah laughed to herself, saying, "After I am worn out, and my lord is old, shall I have pleasure?" The Lord said to Abraham, "Why did Sarah laugh and say, 'Shall I indeed bear a child, now that I am old?' Is anything too hard for the Lord? At the appointed time I will return to you, about this time next year, and Sarah shall have a son." But Sarah denied it, saying, "I did not laugh," for she was afraid. He said, "No, but you did laugh." (Genesis 18:1-15)

Three men come to Abraham's tent. They come on behalf of the Lord, three men representing each of the three God head. Abraham invites them to stay and they do. He gets his house in order to give them food, a big part of their culture. His wife, Sarah, is immediately involved as she makes bread for the guests. When the food is ready, Abraham presents it to them and then stays with them as they eat.

After they have eaten, the men reveal why they have come to Abraham's tent. They immediately ask where Sarah is, and Abraham tells them she is inside the tent. Sarah, being Abraham's wife, had the right to sit with the men as they ate, just like Abraham did, but she stayed in the tent. At this point, when the men ask where she is, she is invited to join the conversation, but once again she stays inside.

The men then say that Sarah will have a son, something that Abraham was already told in Genesis 17. Sarah, listening into the conversation, laughs at the idea. The Lord asks Abraham why Sarah laughed, and Sarah responds, denying it. At this point, the Lord speaks directly to her, asserting that she had indeed laughed.

Sarah keeps herself outside of a conversation she belongs to. Abraham has already been told that Sarah will have a child, so there is no need for him to be told again. These visitors are there to deliver the message to Sarah specifically. When the Lord confronts her that she did indeed laugh, it is not as a rebuke but as a way to engage her in the conversation fully. The Lord tenderly pursues His daughter, drawing her back into the Kingdom.

Sarah has kept herself outside of the Kingdom, involved but not engaged. We see this as she helped make food and stood inside the door of the tent, but did not actively join the conversation. It is likely that she had been disengaged for some time now, and in response the Lord pursues her. He sends men that carry His message and His presence to her home in order to draw her back. He slowly and sweetly brings her into the conversation she was meant to be in.

Being involved isn't the same as being engaged. Being involved is easy; go to Church on Sundays, read the Bible, talk about Jesus. Being engaged takes more; you have to sell out, run with all you have for the Kingdom, and make your personal relationship with Jesus the most important in your life. Involvement does not equal engagement, and what Jesus asks for is full hearted engagement with His Kingdom.

So there's a problem, Kingdom people aren't engaged. They've fallen asleep and become passive and numb to their created home. This is seen throughout the Bible, starting with Adam's passivity as Eve spoke with the serpent, and continues on today. This world groans and aches for the Church to wake up to who She truly is.

We all know the reasons we keep ourselves outside of the Kingdom; fear, lies, heart ache, struggles, pain, the past, and so many other things convince us to stay out of the game. We know this issue well, but we are going to stop talking about the problem. Too often we get bogged down in the issues we face and become lost in the problem. Like in Nascar, if you focus on the wall, you're going to run into the wall.

Instead of focusing on the problem, we are going to be Kingdom minded people and lean into the solution. We are going to choose to practice actively participating in the Kingdom of Heaven.

What you will find here is teaching that will equip you to be Kingdom minded, practical things to do to help in the trials, and empowerment to stand up and be the Church. Because it's time to live the Kingdom life that Christ designed for us. It's time to stop looking at what the world says is possible and to look at Jesus as our example in this life. It's time to step into the things of Eden, the original design for earth. It's time to wake up from our sleep. It's time to engage the Kingdom.

NOTES

1. Matthew 6:33

CPSIA information can be obtained
at www.ICGtesting.com
Printed in the USA
LVOW03s1930050817
543777LV00002B/3/P